SPEAK
OF THE
DEVILS

Published by The Bluecoat Press, Liverpool
Book design by MARCH Graphic Design Studio, Liverpool
Printed by Ashford Colour Press

ISBN 1 904438 49 0

I would like to express my gratitude to the following people who helped in the compilation of this collection as well as the first edition: Mark Baxter, Alan Collings, Richard Jones, Daniel Norcross, Richard Pigden, Warren Shore, Simon Skelly, Mike Spear, James Weber, Theo Weber and Aine Wolstenholme.

SPEAK OF THE DEVILS

The book of
Manchester United
quotations

Compiled by Eugene Weber

The Bluecoat Press

SUCCESS

The success he has had hasn't affected him – but the success he hasn't had has left a mark. He badly wants to win the European Cup, not for himself but for Manchester United. Personally, I think he deserves it for himself.

Joe Mercer, the former Manchester City manager, on Sir Matt Busby in the 1960s.

The moment when Bobby [Charlton] took the Cup it cleansed me. It eased the pain of the guilt of going into Europe. It was my justification.

Sir Matt Busby after winning the European Cup in 1968.

Afterwards, all I can remember is seeing Matt's face at the final whistle. He wasn't crying, but he looked as if he should have had a halo over him. He had one of those faces that lights up, like the pictures you see of saints. He had achieved something that had almost cost him his life.

George Best on the 1968 European Cup win.

And did he look up briefly at the heavens as if seeking – and getting, no doubt – the approval of the spirits of Munich? And did he look too with pride on his bright young men, his hopes for years to come, and maybe more so on Charlton and Foulkes, who had been with him almost since they learned to kick a football? Home are the hunters, home from the hill. At last.

Eric Todd, journalist, on Sir Matt Busby after the 1968 European Cup win

What a lucky guy I am to have been part of this great club success and in my first season too.

Brian Kidd who won his European Cup medal on his 19th birthday.

The only relaxing time, the only time I really enjoyed the game, was in the last few minutes when we were 4-1 up and knew we were going to win. The rest of the game was very tense and afterwards was a terrible anticlimax. When you have been trying to win something so much for someone – a team had died trying to do it – then when you actually achieved it, there was only relief.

Tony Dunne, after the 1968 European Cup final.

There are still some poignant memories. Of going to the all-night banquet at the Russell Hotel and seeing Duncan Edward's parents, and Eddie Colman's parents. All the parents of the Munich victims were invited. I didn't know what to say to them and there were a lot of tears. It was very sad. I kept thinking if he had been alive, Duncan [Edwards] would have been playing instead of me.

Pat Crerand recalling the European Cup win in 1968.

At the end I felt six foot-two tall. Afterwards I took my wife to Danny LaRue's club and had a whale of a time.

Nobby Stiles on the same event.

I think he's on the verge of setting up what we'll look back on and call the Fergie dynasty to match the Busby dynasty.

Wilf McGuinness, the former United player and manager, gives a shrewd assessment after United won the premiership in 1993 – the first in 26 years.

Alex has had to wait seven years for this but I've been waiting for 26.

Martin Edwards, chairman, after the same event.

I must confess when United scored that first goal, I lost all thought of decorum.

Alderman Robert Rodgers, then Lord Mayor of Manchester, after United's first goal in the 1963 FA Cup final against Leicester City.

We were on the 18th green and a man I had never met before walked over the hill and said, 'excuse me, Mr. Ferguson, you are the champions. Oldham have just beaten Villa'.

How Sir Alex Ferguson who found out that United had won the title in 1993 while on the golf course.

When Kevin Moran got sent off and Norman Whiteside got the winner, that was the first time I heard United fans sing, 'always look on the Whiteside of life', which was superb.

Terry Christian, TV personality and United fan.

How appropriate that there should be 39 steps for Buchan to climb to receive the Cup.

↲ ꞌn Motson, commentator, as United captain Martin Buchan climbed the 39 steps at Wembley Stadium to collect the FA Cup in 1977.

It has done my players a world of good to be associated with such a team on the same pitch. But I wish they had suspended Best for five weeks!

Northampton manager Dave Bowen after losing 8-2 to United in the Cup. George Best scored six on his return after four weeks suspension.

Manchester United deserve the trophy every year for having to live and play here.

A Yeovil supporter after his team lost 8-0 to United at Old Trafford in the 1949 FA Cup.

Some people change with success. Some always want to go to Glasgow on holiday. Some want to go to France.

Sir Alex Ferguson.

Fergie Places Shroud Over Turin.
Daily Mail headline after United beat Juventus in the semi-final of the 1999 Champions' League.

None of us are scared because against Juventus, I think we finally proved to ourselves that we have come of age. We're men now, not young boys still learning.
Nicky Butt on the same result.

Only a truly great team could have come back from a 2-0 deficit away from home. Only a truly great team could have rebelled against destiny, against their opponents, against everything. That is what Manchester United achieved on Wednesday night.
La Stampa, Italian newspaper, after the same match.

This United Treble is football's equivalent of Frankie Dettori winning all seven races at Ascot a couple of years ago.
A spokesman for William Hill.

At a time like this you have to lie back and think of England.
The same spokesman.

It can be hell out here in the icy wastes, suffering from the effects of adjectival deprivation. Sometimes you feel like a member of the expeditionary force who must transmit a message to the base-camp quartermaster, 'we are running out of superlatives. Please send reinforcements'. That was the experience at the Stadio Delle Alpi in Turin where the cacophony of approval reached a climax inspired by that supreme Sherpa of footballing ascent, Alex Ferguson.
Nick Townsend, journalist, writing on the same game.

I still haven't worked out how United won the treble. If you think about all the matches they played, it was a fantastic achievement – the kind that happens only once in a century.

Gianluca Vialli, the former Chelsea manager.

The players are brought up as soon as they succeed, to go for the next thing.

Sir Alex Ferguson.

A winner is not always a gentleman.

Sir Alex Ferguson.

Those who accept being in my shadow are the most intelligent people because they know that I make them win.

Eric Cantona.

The biggest thrill I get in football is playing for United when we win at Anfield. It is absolutely magic.

Gary Neville.

We've gone into the lion's den and come out with a trophy. It's a fantastic achievement and I'm proud of all my players.

Sir Alex Ferguson after winning the European Cup Winners's Cup in 1991.

I will be looking forward to walking around London with the medal round my neck and seeing a few Gooners and having a smirk at them.

Teddy Sheringham after the 1999 FA Cup Final win over Newscastle United.

That shuts a few people up. Here's to the Gooners.

Teddy Sheringham after winning the 1999 Double.

I once talked to a Manchester United player about becoming successful and he said, 'the thing for me, Paula, is that there was a moment when I realised it was no more Top Man, but Cecil Gee all the way'.

Paula Yates, showbiz personality.

He's still got to beat my record of 45 goals in 51 games in a season for Dunfermline! Ruud and Ole Gunnar Solskjaer are sick of me going on about it, but I scored 32 League goals in 36 games plus Uefa Cup goals and other Cup games. Ruud scored 44 last season and was one short of my record – that was a shame!

Sir Alex Ferguson.

Victory is an obligation when you play for United and I love that kind of pressure.

Patrice Evra.

Watching that last 15 minutes I thought Arsenal were trying to throw it away! They kept giving the ball away, Chelsea kept driving forward and my heart was in my mouth. But it was a great effort by Chelsea, you have to give them great credit.

Sir Alex Ferguson after winning the Premiership in 2007 when Chelsea needed to beat Arsenal to stay in contention but could only draw at the Emirates stadium.

I am very happy and very proud to get this prize tonight. I would like to say first I owe my success to Manchester United, to my manager Alex Ferguson, my coach Brian Kidd, all my team-mates, the staff, the fans. After that I would like to congratulate other people from football in England, even the players who didn't vote for me, for the pleasure they give me to play in this magnificent football, English football.

Eric Cantona receiving the Player of the Year award in 1994.

That was the biggest roller-coaster of a football match I've ever played in. I went through every single emotion possible. With a minute to go, you've got a penalty and Roy Keane is heading down the tunnel, and you think your name is on the Cup. Well, you would, wouldn't you? Then a gormless Dane pops up and makes a great save. Typical! I think Dennis Bergkamp will still be having nightmares about that penalty. But Ryan Giggs then scored one of the greatest goals I've ever seen. He went round me four or five times!

Lee Dixon on the 1999 FA Cup semi-final.

Football, eh? Bloody hell.

Sir Alex Ferguson after the 1999 Champions' League win.

I'm proud of my players. I'm proud of my family. I'm proud of my heritage and what has been achieved. This is the greatest moment of my life.

Sir Alex Ferguson after the same game.

When I ran on to the pitch at the end I didn't really say anything to any of them. I just hugged and kissed them. I was slobbering all over them because you can't top that. It's the pinnacle.

Sir Alex Ferguson.

The moment at the final whistle was weird. Since I was a youngster I've seen players win the FA Cup and cry and I could never understand it. But as soon as the referee blew the final whistle in the Nou Camp I just went; there was nothing I could do about it.

Ryan Giggs after winning the 1999 Champions' League final.

Just to have been a part of that success against Bayern was an honour. I can remember the tension well. We thought the game was up. Who wouldn't?

Jesper Blomqvist on the same match.

I've won the World Cup but I've never been happier in my life. Solskjaer knocked the ball into the net and I thought, 'this is what paradise is all about'.

Sir Bobby Charlton after Champions' League final win.

I can't believe it. I can't believe it. Bloody hell.

Sir Alex Ferguson.

Matt Busby would have been 90 yesterday. It must have been Dick Turpin's birthday as well.

Alex Stepney on the same result.

For many people the most enduring memory of that night was the sight of the Bayern players collapsing to the ground in tears, their devastation the result of our last-minute goals. Even among our fans there was some sympathy, but that sympathy did not extend to the United dressing room. We had beaten them the way Germans tend to beat everyone else.

Jaap Stam after the Champions' League win.

Tactics didn't win that game last night. It was sheer will, maybe luck, too. They never stopped and you have to give them credit for that. For that equaliser we had nine bodies in the box.

Sir Alex Ferguson on the Champions League final.

After what we've done and the way we played, people have to admire us even if they don't like us.

Gary Neville after the same match

With Manchester United, it is never over until the Fat Lady has had a heart attack.

Hugh McIlvanney, journalist, on the 1999 Champions' League final.

Even when we got back in the dressing room and we were almost out of control with delight, I don't think any of us could really take it in. What I remember most was the feeling that what we had done actually meant something, it had affected peoples' lives.

Gary Neville.

The Germans were getting flashy. It gave me the hump.

Teddy Sheringham, who scored the equaliser in the Champions' League final.

Two Subs Went On, Torpedoes Away.

The Daily Mail on the Champions League final win.

He's brought me up, he's made my career. He deserves everything he gets and we owe it all to him.

David Beckham on Sir Alex Ferguson after United won the 1999 Champions' League.

Don't you dare come back in here without having done your best.

Part of Alex Ferguson's half-time team talk during the 1999 Champions' League final.

The Cup is only six feet away from you at the end of this day. If you lose, you can't even touch it.

More of Sir Alex Ferguson's half-time pep talk.

I just thought it might be my night. I called one of my friends and told him he better watch the game. I always call him when I have this feeling.

Ole Gunnar Solskjaer.

Whatever Arsenal or Chelsea or, let's be kind, Liverpool, can conjure up, they will simply be reduced to being second man on the Moon.

Danny Baker, journalist.

I truly believed the Treble was romance, nor reality.

Sir Alex Ferguson after winning the 1999 Champions' League and the Treble.

The time was up and I looked round and saw the Cup was on its way down and it had Bayern Munich colours on it. Two minutes later I had it in my own hands.

David Beckham.

The two minutes transcend sport. It demeans the occasion to describe it merely as 'dramatic'. 'Sensational' similarly sounds hollow. No, this was politics, it was history, it was art, it was destiny. It was an object lesson in life.

Jonathan Margolis, journalist, after United won the 1999 Champions' League.

You can't buy moments like that – Ireland would have to win the World Cup to match it.

Denis Irwin after United won the 1999 Champions' League.

If anyone still wonders why I stayed at Manchester United they can see here why. Team spirit is unbelievable.

Ole Gunnar Solskjaer after United won the 1999 Champions' League.

I was starting to adjust to defeat near the end. I kept saying to myself, 'keep your dignity and accept it's not your year'.

Sir Alex Ferguson after winning the 1999 Champions' League.

MISBEHAVING

When the boss calls you into his office you know you're for it. He doesn't hand out the toffees.
Nobby Stiles on Sir Matt Busby.

Denis [Law] once kicked me at Wembley in front of the Queen in an international. I mean, no man is entitled to do that, really
Sir Bobby Robson.

I was up in his office a few times when I was a kid and he could be stern. You didn't mess about with him, but I think he liked a bit of devilment. He'd be telling you off, but he'd have a glint in his eye.
Nobby Stiles on Sir Matt Busby.

When Matt Busby sent for me I used to look at the wallpaper behind his head. It was funny wallpaper with animals on and I used to count the animals while he gave me a bollocking. I used to want the bollocking to last a long time so I could finish my counting. One day he got really mad at me and went on at some length and I managed to count them all. There are 272 animals on Matt Busby's wallpaper.
George Best.

I have lost my temper before and I will do it again. I suppose in the old days I tended to hit first and then think later. Now I think before I hit.
Roy Keane.

I suppose my crime sheet makes me appear to be something of an old lag. It's certainly nothing to boast about. But all my sins have been in retaliation. I've never been a dirty player. Perhaps, I've been too easily provoked, like many Scots.
Pat Crerand.

How sweet that Arsenal manager Arsene Wenger should say Manchester United's David Beckham deserved to be sent off for his foul on Necaxa's Jose Milian during the World Club Championship in Brazil. Most remarkable. It must be the first red-card incident Wenger has managed to see with his own eyes in years.

Kate Battersby, journalist.

As for the sending off, well Jason McAteer would annoy anybody.

Roy Keane after being sent off for elbowing Sunderland's McAteer.

We can't all be a Bobby Charlton.

Sir Alex Ferguson on his temperament.

All I could see was the ball. I thought I had a 50-50 chance of getting it.

Kevin Moran on the tackle that led him to be the first player to be sent off in an FA Cup final – in 1985 against Everton.

A lot of people are afraid to ask me about being sent off in that match. What they forget about is that it never really bothered me being sent off because we won the game. If we had lost the game I think that even now I'd feel a bit sick.

Kevin Moran.

I don't think that because someone is sent off in a Cup final he should be regarded as a total embarrassment to the game. But that is how I felt.

Kevin Moran.

I don't care if he's George Best or Pele. Unless he's willing to do hard training, he won't get a look in.

Malcolm Holman, manager of the Ford Open Prison football team, after Best's arrival to start a three-month sentence for drunk driving.

15

Norman's goal really lifted us. It was a brilliant goal and in many ways when I look back on the final, even though my dismissal got a lot of coverage, it was a shame really because the whole thing about the game should have been Norman's.

Kevin Moran, on Norman Whiteside who scored the winner for United in the 1985 FA Cup final.

Call it arrogance, call it craziness, call it petulance. But Cantona is Cantona. Like me, outbursts such as this are in the blood. I never went looking for trouble and I'm sure Eric doesn't either. Trouble just finds you.

Denis Law after Eric Cantona's attack on a fan at Crystal Palace.

I'll never change my game. It isn't possible. If I did I wouldn't be half the player I am. I'd be back in Irish football. I'll obviously be sent off a few more times. It's part and parcel of the game.

Roy Keane.

He reminds me of [Bryan] Robson in many ways but does not have the control in the tackle in terms of not getting booked. Robbo would get away with murder and even argue with refs – he was good at that. Roy can't. Robbo had it down to a fine art and withdrew before the ref reached for his card. Roy carries on and gets the card.

Sir Alex Ferguson on Roy Keane.

I don't think anyone in the history of football will get the sentence Eric got, unless they had killed Bert Millichip's dog.

Sir Alex Ferguson on Eric Cantona's eight-month ban by the FA for his kung-fu attack on a fan at Crystal Palace.

It is fortunate that most players are not like me or there would be anarchy.

Eric Cantona.

George Best was provoked all the time but he handled it. We were brought up to believe that when playing for Manchester United you don't worry about the crowd.

Alex Stepney reacting to Eric Cantona's kung-fu attack on a fan at Crystal Palace.

Wasn't it good to see Eric Cantona back in action? Let's hope this time he remembers that kicking people in the teeth is the Tory government's job.

Tony Blair MP, then Leader of the Opposition, after Cantona's return from suspension.

I've been punished for striking a goalkeeper. For spitting at supporters. For throwing my shirt at a referee. For calling my manager a bag of shit. I called those who judged a bunch of idiots. I thought I might have trouble finding a sponsor.

Eric Cantona in an advertisement for Nike.

It's shameful – poor Eric might as well commit suicide

Cantona's mother after he received a two-week prison sentence for his kung-fu attack on a Crystal Palace fan. The sentence was commuted to community service on appeal.

Try not to foul.

Eric Cantona while training youngsters.

Fair play to Eric. I might have done the same myself. Of course, when I got home and saw the television pictures I could see it was a nasty incident. Out of order, too. But my attitude didn't change. My heart went out to him and all the lads felt the same.

Roy Keane.

I definitely think we were unfairly treated over Cantona and Keane. It makes me laugh when people go on about so-called incidents our players have been involved in this past year and you see some of the tackles that go on in other games. There's not been one broken nose, broken jaw, cut, gash, knee ligament injury or even a bled wart, not a flippin' thing as a result of our players' tackles.

Sir Alex Ferguson.

We are no longer prepared to tolerate his wayward behaviour. If he got married and settled down, it would help somewhat. But his present behaviour has got to stop. One thing we have to understand is that George Best is a genius. The problem is that he has had as much adulation as Pele of Brazil and he got it very young. He has been continually hounded by the press and public alike and his weakness for a pretty girl has not helped the situation.

Sir Matt Busby.

Hopefully, I won't be sent off as captain, but if I was a betting man, I wouldn't have much money on that.

Roy Keane.

Hard men are nothing new in football. In my young days there were quite a few killers about, men who went in for rough play and intimidation. But you wouldn't expect one team to have more than a couple of them. What is new and frightening about the present situation is that you have entire sides that have physical hardness as their main asset.

Sir Matt Busby in 1969.

The Boss never has to say anything. If any member of the staff does anything wrong, the other players are so ashamed of him because he has let down the Boss, that the lad goes along and apologises.

Jack Crompton, who was the United goalkeeper between 1944 and '56.

Do they seriously think I don't want to change? Of course I do!.
But I can't change. I know myself well enough to realise I can't
promise to change. I can only try and go on trying. I can get
whacked from the back or hit when the ball has gone 28 times in a
row and do nothing or say nothing. I don't know why it should boil
the 29th time, which has been no different. It just happens.
George Best.

Why can't he have been like Tom Finney?
John Anthony, journalist, on George Best.

If a fellow has to kick me it means he is not as good as I am.
George Best.

Nobby doesn't so much tackle people as bump into them.
Sir Bobby Charlton on Nobby Stiles.

We were probably playing against the world, Mars and everyone
else tonight.
**Alex Ferguson after Eric Cantona was sent off for the second time in
four days in the 2-2 draw at Arsenal in 1994.**

The first wasn't a foul, so I thought, if they want a foul I'll give
them a foul.
Eric Cantona after he was sent off at Arsenal in 1994.

He's a sensitive lad and he appreciates the mistake he has made.
He shouldn't be thrown to the wolves.
Sir Bobby Charlton on David Beckham after the same event.

I would ask our fans to be fair to him. He made a mistake but I saw a lot worse in the World Cup than what he did.

Arsene Wenger before the Charity Shield clash against Manchester United and David Beckham's first competitive match since being sent off in the World Cup

I have been horrified to hear and read about what has happened to Beckham since I sent him off. It's unbelievable how this boy has been vilified. We are talking only about football, not the Third World War.

Kim Milton Nielsen, the referee who sent David Beckham off in the World Cup.

This sort of lynch-mob mentality is not only highly dangerous, but totally unfair. It makes me mad – it's just incredible.

Diego Simeone, who was involved in the clash which resulted in David Beckham being sent off in the 1998 World Cup.

Simeone has got a lot of people sent off, not just Beckham – I think it was more Simeone's fault than Beckham's. Beckham is Beckham. He doesn't have to prove anything to anyone. It isn't easy to play against Simeone, you know.

Gabriel Batistuta, Argentina striker and team-mate of Diego Simeone.

I was sent off for pushing him but if you're going to get sent off, you might as well punch him properly. It's the same punishment. You might as well get hung for a sheep as a lamb.

Roy Keane on being sent off against Newcastle for pushing Alan Shearer.

When I get kicked I'm supposed to count to ten and then walk away. I can't. If a player deliberately kicks me, I'll kick him back.

Denis Law.

It's amazing. If he had come in here a few years ago he would have been lynched. If he paid a visit now he wouldn't be allowed to buy a drink all night and everyone would treat him like a hero.

The landlord of the the Pleasant Pheasant pub in South Norwood, London, after David Beckham scored against Greece to ensure England qualified for the 2002 World Cup. When Beckham was sent off at the 1998 World Cup customers at the pub hung an effigy of Beckham outside the premises.

I would like our supporters to be sure of one thing: if there were any danger of one of our players dabbling in any kind of drug, be it to enhance his performance or for his social life, he would be quickly gone from United. Be assured the manager, his coaches and medical staff would know. Believe me, we have nothing like that at Old Trafford.

Sir Alex Ferguson.

Some of my best players over the years like Robson, Keane, Ince, Hughes, Butt and Scholes have flirted with the worst of the game that brings them yellow and red cards. What I have always tried to do is make them understand we have a reputation. And the reputation of this club has been good over the years considering the number of competitive games we play and the expectation surrounding us. I remember a time when we had four players sent off in two months – Cantona twice, Kanchelskis, Hughes and Schmeichel. I called them in, gave them an ultimatum and quietened them down.

Sir Alex Ferguson.

I expected the ref to award a free kick against me. But when he didn't, I wasn't going to argue.

Nat Lofthouse, who scored in the 1958 Cup final against United after shoulder-charging Harry Gregg and the ball into the net.

A goal should never have been awarded. I remember sitting seething in the bath at Wembley praying that Lofthouse wouldn't retire before I had a chance to get my own back. I'm happy to tell you that he didn't and I did.

Harry Gregg.

Here Harry, this one's free. We don't charge goalkeepers here.

Nat Lofthouse, years later, to Harry Gregg when he visited Lofthouse's pub.

It was never dirty. Not like when Jimmy Case, Graeme Souness, Whiteside and Robbo were going at each other a few years back in these fixtures. You had to make sure your mummy was sitting beside you then, because you couldn't watch it alone. Today they just got stuck in.

Alex Ferguson after United's last-minute win over Liverpool in the 4th round of the 1999 FA Cup.

I'd waited long enough. I f***ing hit him hard. The ball was there (I think). 'Take that, you c***'. I didn't wait for the [red] card. I turned and walked to the dressing room.

Roy Keane describing his tackle on Manchester City's Alf-Inge Haaland.

John Fitzpatrick, a young Manchester United player who had acquired a reputation for being an up-and-coming hard man, was warned that he should stay away from me. But the word was he had not taken the hint. So when a 50-50 ball came along, it was seen by both of us as a matter of survival that we got in the first strike. I did, and it may well have contributed to ending his career. At the time I didn't feel guilt because, in my 'blinkered' world, it had been a simple matter of self-preservation.

Johnny Giles, the former Leeds United midfielder.

VERBALS

All I know is that I'll never be able to achieve what Tommy did and that is take Aston Villa into the Third Division, and better than that, take Manchester United into the Second Division.
Ron Atkinson on Tommy Docherty.

Best has given footballers a bad name and I saw it as my job to repair their reputation. It took a long time and a lot of hard work, but I like to think I helped.
Kevin Keegan.

He's not fit to lace my boots as a player.
George Best on Kevin Keegan.

Keegan is not fit to lace George Best's drinks.
John Roberts, journalist

He can't run, he can't tackle and he can't head a ball. The only time he goes forward is to toss the coin.
Tommy Docherty on Ray Wilkins.

Quite honestly, if England played in my back garden I'd close the curtains.
George Best in 1970.

The present United side would have beaten the Sixties team 10-0.
Peter Schmeichel.

Peter's got a fair point. After all, we're all over fifty now.
Nobby Stiles.

The BBC are dying for us to lose. Everyone is from Liverpool with a supporter's badge.

Sir Alex Ferguson.

He wears No.10. I thought it was his position but it turns out to be his IQ.

George Best on Paul Gascoigne.

Roy Keane thinks he's a hard man. Lock him up in a cell with another con, a knife each and no clothes on. Then we'll see how hard he is.

'Mad' Frankie Fraser, former criminal, who spent more than half his life in prison for various offences.

I used to say he was a great asset to television because they didn't need slow motion when he was on the ball.

Denis Law on Pat Crerand.

SCHOLES

He's a man's man. You look at him and say. 'he would never rat on anyone'.

Sir Alex Ferguson.

The best United player is Paul Scholes. He is the most talented of them all. He knows how to dribble, can pass well, can score and he is quick around the pitch. If you have all those four things, and not many players do, then you have to be one of the best around.

Robert Pires, the former Arsenal midfielder.

Paul Scholes is just about the best player of his kind I have ever seen. He has got energy, courage, a real eye for a goal and he wants to win. Those four things make him a great player.

Eyal Berkovic.

I love little Scholes. He is my type of player. He wants to score and it hurts when it doesn't. He will have the ball all the time. I used to feel like that myself. I hated playing on the wing, I was always criticised for coming in but I had to because I didn't get enough of the ball. I see that with Scholes. He also has a fantastic technique. He reminds me of myself. If somebody threw the ball at me I would just do it. No-one taught me, it's instinct, something you can't change. He's the same. I love watching him play.

Sir Bobby Charlton.

Paul Scholes could play in a five-a-side with a blindfold on, he just knows where everything is. If he played centre-half he might struggle heading the ball but he would football his way out of trouble. He is what I'd call a proper footballer.

Mick Brown, retiring chief scout.

All the managers I speak to love Scholes. They think he's a great player. He has that little trick to beat men, he's a good deliverer of the ball, two-footed, scores and his ghosting into the box is exceptional.

Sir Alex Ferguson.

People don't rate Scholes as they should. For me, he's the best English player by far. He's miles better than anyone else. He scores, has vision and puts his foot in.

Thierry Henry.

As for Scholes, I love to watch him play. I think he's a terrific player. And I admire him because he is so quiet outside the football life. You never hear anything about him, like Zidane. I like that. That's what I call a big player.

Patrick Vieira.

There is not a player in the land as good as he is. He has control, composure, vision, awareness. He is absolutely magnificent and for me one of the greatest players in the game.

Sir Alex Ferguson.

Gary Neville was having a piss one day, 45 yards away by the fence. Scholes whacked him right in the arse.

Sir Alex Ferguson on Scholes's long-range shooting abilities.

What I like most about Paul, though, is that he is the epitome of a professional footballer. He comes to training, then goes home and spends his time with his family. He doesn't like all the hoo-ha outside the football, the interviews with papers and on TV. He prefers to just live his own life and he refuses to be a media object or a public figure. I have nothing but admiration for him.

Ruud van Nistelrooy.

ROONEY

Rooney is very special and has a brilliant future. He has so much skill and talent. You don't have to be Brazilian to have a Brazilian talent.

Carlos Alberto, captain of the Brazil side that won the World Cup in 1970.

Wayne Rooney's so strong he can do anything. He would be the ideal person to help you move house.

Michel Salgado, the Real Madrid defender.

He is the biggest English talent I have seen since I took over at Highbury. He is supposed to be 16 but I didn't know 16-year-olds could do things like that. He is everything you could dream of; intelligence, quick reactions, strong running with the ball. You can put him in the centre, you can put him on the wing, you can play him behind the striker.

Arsene Wenger.

He has the potential to be a legendary player. One of Pele's great qualities was that he could take any situation in his stride. From the little I have seen of Wayne, I think he can do that, too. Great players always have the habit of being able to rise to the occasion. Like Pele used to, they puff out their chests and show the world who is in charge.

Zico, the former Brazilian legend.

It was like seeing your missus in bed with another fella.

Everton fan as Rooney began his United career with a brilliant hat-trick against Turkish team Fenerbahce in the Champions' League.

Is he as good as me? Now don't be silly!

George Best after Wayne Rooney's debut for United.

He's Scholesy with a finish. I know Paul does get a few but he's not prolific like Rooney.

Denis Law.

Having reported on Manchester United for the past 46 years, I have witnessed the first games in a red shirt of numerous players destined to become household names, from the near-holy trinity of Charlton, Law and Best, through to Eric Cantona and David Beckham. But no-one has strutted his stuff with the same panache as Wayne Rooney displayed against Fenerbahce.

David Meek, journalist.

It will be pressure 24 hours a day, seven days a week. If you go out for a beer, all of a sudden it's multiplied by 12. If you're seen walking down the road with a girl you're having an affair.

Norman Whiteside on Rooney.

You don't make an assessment like this lightly. You think of all the great players you have seen or played with and against, from Di Stefano through Pele to Zidane, and you remind yourself of all that they had, what made them unique in their time, and then you look at this kid Rooney, who at first glance doesn't even look like a player. And when you do that over a certain length of time you don't see some lumpy prodigy who might for one reason or another burn out very quickly. You see a beautiful flower of a talent, perfectly formed.

Johnny Giles.

Wayne Rooney is a phenomenal talent and has already achieved a lot. He could go on to be as great as Bobby Charlton and help England win the World Cup.

Maradona.

If I were to praise one thing, it was his attitude. He is 18 and he knows all eyes are on him but he goes out and does his own thing. To do that at his young age is fantastic

Ruud van Nistelrooy on Rooney's debut for United.

If there is one player in this England team capable of inspiring the nation it's Rooney – and without him we are doomed. I would go as far as to say that if anything happens to him prior to the finals I'd be of a mind to not even go to Germany because we wouldn't have a chance, believe me.

Terry Butcher, the former England defender, before the 2006 World Cup.

The masses will always be with guys like Roon, not with the straight guy. What they do with him is they take a kid and they tell him, 'be a kid, but act grown up'. How are you going to do that? Sport is all about immaturity. That's why guys stay in it too long because they want to stay children.

Mike Tyson.

It's hard to put into words. He's done it in the European Championship with England and now in the Champions League with Manchester United. Honestly, I don't think he knows the word 'pressure' – it can't be in his vocabulary.

Rio Ferdinand.

UNITED

A United player is a passionate mix of skill, heart and youth. Manchester United are all about flair and improvisation; a club with history and style bred on romance.

Harry Gregg.

Old Trafford is the theatre of dreams.

Sir Bobby Charlton.

Manchester United stands for something more than any person, any player, any supporter. It is the 'soul' of a sporting organisation which goes on season after season, making history all the time.
United programme notes from 1937.

'Keep off the Grass' signs were in six languages. It ain't exactly what we're used to.
Harry Redknapp arriving at Old Trafford with Portsmouth for an FA Cup tie in 2003.

The main difference is that United is a real football club with a great history, whereas Barcelona is more like a political movement representing the eight million people of Catalonia, a government, even.
Jordi Cruyff, who played for United and Barcelona.

I don't want to be anyone's assistant, but I'd go to Manchester United as kit manager.
Sammy Mcilroy.

It's a love story, it's a love story
Eric Cantona on his relationship with United.

The great tradition of the club is most obvious when we travel away, especially when we go abroad. Everyone seems to know us and the name of the club is treated with respect. We always take care to dress as smartly as possible because we are representing Manchester United.
Brian Greenhoff.

The club is a kind of reversal of the city's fate. Through it the lost capital city of the industrial revolution is reborn.
Fintan O'Toole, journalist.

There are parts of the world where Manchester United are the only English words the natives know.

Eamon Dunphy, journalist and former United youth player.

Manchester United plc? It means Premier League champions, of course.

Terry Christian, TV personality and United fan.

It's the biggest club in Norway

Ole Gunnar Solskjaer.

Old Trafford is the only stadium in the world that's absolutely buzzing with atmosphere when it's empty. It's almost like a cathedral.

Tommy Docherty.

I give you the answer in three words: skill, fitness and character and the greatest of these is character.

Sir Matt Busby on the key attributes of a Manchester United player.

He didn't just act as if it was his ball. He acted as if it was his stadium.

Pat Crerand on Denis Law.

My Dad tells me that I've always wanted to play here. He said when I first saw Old Trafford I just stood and stared for an hour.

Gary Neville.

It's like being in a palace, an overwhelming and inspiring place. Even the loos have gold taps.

Garry Birtles.

To have a criticism of Old Trafford is almost impossible. When you're there, you're the envy of all the other players in the football league. You're playing in the best stadium in the country, you've got the biggest and best support you could hope for. How could anyone that's been there slag it off?

Lou Macari.

Old Trafford is a theatre for entertainment, drama and football spectacle. It's not a stadium where you should hear bellyaching or fans bickering about their own team. That just destroys the magic of the place.

Ron Atkinson.

There was David Beckham clearing away his dishes after breakfast in the canteen and thanking the tea lady. We learned a great deal.

Francois Pinnaar, then coach of the Saracens rugby union club, after a fact finding mission to Old Trafford.

It's the club of my life. When I die, I have asked for my ashes to be scattered on the Old Trafford turf.

Eric Cantona.

TRAGEDY

A man in dungarees – which on the Old Trafford terraces is a kind of supporter's uniform – came into the public bar and said, 'I still can't credit it'. He pulled a bundle of programme vouchers out of his pocket – representing all the season's games he had seen – and threw them down irritably. 'There, best team in the blinkin' world'.

A United supporter after the Munich disaster.

At six o'clock out of pure curiosity, I turned on my television set. As the news came on the screen seemed to go black. The normally urbane voice of the announcer seemed to turn into a sledge-hammer. I sat listening with a frozen brain to that cruel and shocking list of casualties that was now to give to the word Munich an even sadder meaning than it had acquired on a day before the war when a British Prime Minister had come home to London waving a pitiful piece of paper and most of us knew that new calamities of war were inevitable.

H.E. Bates, writer.

At first I thought I was the only one left. I could not realise I was alive myself. In fact I thought I was dreaming.

Harry Gregg after the Munich air crash.

Yesterday on Munich airfield, Association football shrank to a small matter.

The Guardian newspaper.

Even if it means being heavily defeated we will carry on with the season's programme. We have a duty to the public.

Harold Hardman, the Manchester United chairman.

The moment Manchester United took the field the plainsong rose from the ground. One has heard a roar on many fields and in many parts but never one like that. In it there was a proud defiance, turning away any sympathy or mercy and from that moment life was blown into the embers of the night.

The Times newspaper on the same game.

Before the start the crowd of 60,000 stood in silence for a minute in memory of those who died in Munich. This solemnity dissolved in a roar of welcome when the United team, led by Foulkes, the new captain, ran onto the field. Foulkes and Gregg, the goalkeeper, two survivors of the crash, were warmly cheered for almost everything they did throughout the game. It seemed gallant of them to be there at all and much more than that to play as spiritedly as they did. With the cheers of welcome was mingled a kind of sigh, as though a weight had been lifted. Then came the final whistle. The crowd moved like a sea under the floodlights, shaking with their own cheers.

The Guardian newspaper on United's game against Sheffield Wednesday, the first match after the Munich disaster.

Sheffield Wednesday had no chance, and I felt sorry for them. I don't think they had any heart for the fight. The crowd was hysterical and I was not far off being the same way.

Bill Foulkes on the same game, which United won 3-0.

I was lost and sorrowing, and for a short period utterly defeated. A man's help at such a time is not his experience, but his faith and the love and encouragement of his friends.

Sir Matt Busby.

I wasn't hurt. I wasn't even deeply troubled in mind. I just couldn't take it in, and therefore it washed over me. I didn't want to accept what happened.

Sir Bobby Charlton.

It would have been as pointless for me to ask the pilot if everything was okay as if he had asked me whether I had picked the best team for Manchester United.

Sir Matt Busby replying when asked why he not refused to travel on the plane back from Munich.

34

Sometimes I still see them play.

Sir Matt Busby.

The surgeons felt he might live but no one except those close to him ever felt he would be a force again in football. But I knew. In one of his conscious moments he waved a feeble hand for me to come to his side. I had to bend low over his bed to catch his words, 'keep the flag flying, Jimmy. Keep things going until I get back'.

Jimmy Murphy, Sir Matt Busby's assistant.

I know it sounds terrible but my career must have been helped by that tragedy. I mean, how could I have displaced anyone like Eddie Colman.? He was a genius.

Nobby Stiles.

Before it happened I could see ten years ahead, ten years at the top. After it, I had two choices, either to lie down and hide, or pick up the challenge. My wife Jean and the people of Manchester made the decision for me.

Sir Matt Busby.

At first I felt I was going out of my mind, not knowing where to start.

Jimmy Murphy in the immediate aftermath of the Munich disaster when he had to run the club.

I'll never forget it. I came home right away and confirmed it. I didn't know what to think, I was numb. I had sent Liam Whelan over there and the hardest thing I ever had to do was to go over and meet his mother. I knew he was dead but I wasn't sure she knew or not. When I went over it was terrible. They were a lovely family

Billy Behan, United's Ireland scout.

Matt was at death's door but when he started to get well I went over to see him to tell him I was retiring, told him I couldn't face sending a player away any more. But he said, 'well, how do you think I feel?' And I said, 'it's like this, Matt, you're the strand, I'm only a grain of sand on the strand, don't start comparing me with you'. But he said, 'we think you're more than that'. So I said I would stay as long as he stayed.

Billy Behan.

If the worst happens, I am ready for death. I hope we all are.

Liam Whelan's last words.

My wife Jean says I'm bitter, but I don't think so really. I became depressed and did nothing for a couple of years. It was not that I couldn't do anything. I just did not want to do anything.

Jackie Blanchflower after retiring because of injuries sustained in the Munich crash.

The kids who follow United now are fanatics, but I believe that fanaticism stemmed from that day in Munich. A team died but I believe a club was born.

Albert Scanlon, who was injured in the crash.

I am a Catholic. I have always believed in the afterlife, but what was an afterlife to those lads? What power was it that could allow them to be destroyed? It had shaken my faith. I was very mixed up in the mind. I was absolutely certain that I would have no more to do with football. I didn't want to see anyone who had the remotest connection with the game. I was horrible to live with.

Sir Matt Busby.

I want the best team in the country again – and I'll have it.

Sir Matt Busby to Dennis Viollet.

The word 'great' is used too lightly these days. You only have to turn on the television to see a 'great' pass, pick up a paper to read about a 'great' game, switch on the radio to hear about a 'great' goal. They can't all be great. But the Busby Babes were great. Great players, a great team, great people. Great days. Their death stunned the world. No just Manchester, not just Lancashire, not just Britain. The world.

Nat Lofthouse, the former Bolton Wanderers and England striker.

I doubt whether Real Madrid would have won as much as they did if that United side had survived.

Sir Bobby Charlton.

I always felt as if we were cheating somehow. Stepping into other people's shoes. I felt in a way I shouldn't have been there.

Ian Greaves, who came into the United team after Munich.

I often think about that time and the team we had in the 1950s. And I love talking about it, because it gives me pleasure not sadness.

Wilf McGuinness, the former United player and manager.

Everything began to go wrong after Munich. It was like throwing a pebble in the water, the ripples just spread and spread.

Elizabeth, wife of Ray Wood who survived the crash.

He carried the scar of Munich with him for the rest of his life, I believe. But it was a measure of his greatness that he built the greatness of United again.

Jackie Blanchflower, who survived the Munich crash, on Sir Matt Busby.

One of my earliest memories of Manchester United is the catastrophic Munich air disaster. I was six and did not fully understand at the time why a deep gloom prevailed in our house as the news of the tragedy filtered through.

Bertie Ahern, prime minister of the Irish Republic.

Although we mourn our dead and grieve for our wounded we believe that our great days are not done for us. The sympathy and encouragement of the football world, and particularly our supporters, will justify and inspire us. The road back may be long and hard but with the memory of those who died at Munich, of their stirring achievements and wonderful sportsmanship ever with us, MANCHESTER UNITED WILL RISE AGAIN.

Harold Hardman, United chairman, in his programme notes for United's first game after the Munich disaster.

Don't make me out to be John Wayne. I'm not John Wayne, I don't want to play John Wayne.

Harry Gregg, who returned to the burning plane and rescued some of his team-mates as well as other passengers.

Twice I had been given the last rites of the Roman Catholic Church. I just wanted to stay inside the [oxygen] tent and die there, rather than come out of it and learn the truth. So I prayed for the end to come quickly.

Sir Matt Busby.

All gone in a second. Just like that. This has had a permanent effect on me. I find myself waiting for the next blow to fall. I am apprehensive all the time.

Sir Matt Busby.

I want to be, and try to be, a better man than I was before the crash, but I don't think I am.

Sir Matt Busby.

It was a nightmare, with mangled wreckage and bodies lying in the snow. I felt terribly angry at what happened. I just wanted to dash into the wrecked plane, find the pilot and attack him.

Dennis Viollet.

Many things tormented me about that day, and still do – 46 years later. Life's a bitch. But I'm one of the lucky ones.

Harry Gregg.

Obviously life had changed and it would never be the same again for anyone at the club. It wasn't for yourself any more; you weren't trying to build a career or anything like that. You were giving everything you had for Manchester United and the lads who didn't make it at Munich.

Sir Bobby Charlton.

TEAM SPIRIT

In Korea if a player makes a mistake, the other players don't like to point it out, rather they try to embrace it, they take the attitude, 'let's do better next time'. But in the West if you do something wrong another player will make a point of saying something and you will have to fix it immediately.

Park Ji-Sung.

We have the squad rotation thing at United and I always say that it's good, we need that, but if you're not in the team, well, f*** the squad rotation.

Roy Keane.

In my business, togetherness is not just a nice concept that you can take or leave according to taste. If you don't have it, you are nothing. Selfishness, factionalism, cliquishness are all death to a football team.

Sir Alex Ferguson

I don't see team-mates as competitors. I always feel we are part of the team. If my role is to play minutes, that's my role. If I'm on the bench to encourage, that's my role. If I'm just being in the squad, that's my role. We've got fantastic strikers at Old Trafford, a blend now of young and experienced players. The squad is very strong.

Ole Gunnar Solskjaer.

We have never been a side who have come out in the papers and said things about each other or other players.

David Beckham.

There's a lot more calmness, not as much panic really when Eric is playing. He can come into midfield, bring people into the game. Whereas, when he was not playing, we were rushing it a bit.

Ryan Giggs.

I have never been interested in simply sending out a collection of brilliant individuals. There is no substitute for talent but, on the field, talent without unity of purpose is a hopelessly devalued currency.

Sir Alex Ferguson.

So far in my 25 and a half years, I've never complained to a manager who picks a team without me. He wants the team to win. So when he wants me to do a job, I'm prepared.

Ole Gunnar Solskjaer

It is great to look around the changing room and think, 'I'm glad to have him in my side, and him and him'. In fact there is no one who I would doubt.

David Beckham.

It's the collective part of the team that is important. If I'd wanted to draw attention to myself I'd have played singles tennis or chosen a nice lady for mixed doubles.

Eric Cantona.

He has a special role in the team and the squad. Gary keeps the group together, day and night. He makes sure there is a great atmosphere all the time. He is not so much the funny man, but I see him as the binding factor. He is the one who organises everything for the players and their wives. He is such a warm and social person. He does a kind of team building, which is fantastic for a club and must be fantastic too for the boss.

Ruud van Nistelrooy on Gary Neville.

If you go to any office, not everyone is going to like each other. It is the same at United. Not everyone is pals. I don't think I've ever given any of them my phone number.

Roy Keane.

You can't be an avant-gardist in football. It's a team game.

Eric Cantona

I love Manchester United. I would watch them three times a day if they were on television that often. I always hope they can win simply because of the way they play. And because they work really hard for each other. They have won so much and yet they've still got so much desire to win. I admire that.

Gianluca Vialli, the former Chelsea manager.

Good players don't always make good teams.

Roy Keane.

In our football years, we are strong because we're all in the same boat and we are in danger. We work together to survive, then when you quit, you don't have that goal any more. You're not on that boat and you are left with only the memory. What you know is that you will never live again like you have lived on that boat. That is a frustration because what you had was so strong.

Eric Cantona.

I have seen United players getting complacent, thinking they've done it all and getting carried away by a bit of success. All you have to do is drop your standards by five or 10 per cent and it's obvious, especially in Europe. You can carry maybe one player, but no more than that.

Roy Keane.

TACTICS

When a team has international players like Denis Law, Bobby Charlton and George Best in attack, they have their own ideas and it is a waste of talent to subject them to a list of do's and don'ts.

Sir Matt Busby.

Let me say, here and now, that I do not believe in tactics. There is a lot of rot talked by a lot of people about tactics and coaching. These are the people who wear their lapel badges to boost their ego, take their holidays at Lilleshall and talk of the coaching manual as if it was a football bible.

George Best.

If one day, all the tacticians reached perfection, the result would be a 0-0 draw and there would be nobody there to see it.

Pat Crerand

You can never judge what the opposition is likely to do. Any plans should be based on the skill of your own players in adapting.

Sir Matt Busby.

The good coaches are the ones who can get the most out of their players. Tactics, 4-4-2, 3-5-2, for me this is a lot of bollocks. You play the tactics that suit your players and give you the best chance of winning a game but getting the best out of your players is really what gets you results. In that area Ferguson's brilliant. Not only has he got that inbuilt winning mentality, he knows his players like his own children.

Laurent Blanc.

You need an O-level or a degree to understand the tactics at Old Trafford.

Gordon Hill, United winger in the 1970s, after leaving United when Dave Sexton was manager.

Balloon ball. The percentage game. Route one. It has crept into the First Division. We get asked to loan youngsters to these teams. We don't do it. They come back with bad habits, big legs and good eyesight.

Ron Atkinson.

Brian Clough's advice to me before most games was, 'you get it, you pass it to another player in a red shirt'. That's really all I've tried to do at Forest and United – pass and move – and I've made a career out of it.

Roy Keane.

The fundamentals of the game are the same today as they were in my playing days; it is my aim to make footballers out of my boys, and if I succeed, the tactics are comparatively easy to solve.

Sir Matt Busby.

We were not a tactical side. We just played. We should have won more than we did.

Tony Dunne.

SIR MATT

Everything that's been said about Matt since he died was said before he died. That's the greatest epitaph that he could have.

Willie Morgan, the former United winger.

Today's a sad day. I never met him but I saw him thousands of times. He loved everyone – he must have done to put up with George Best.

Doreen Catterall, a United supporter, at Sir Matt Busby's funeral.

Sir Matt Busby's gift for leadership owed much to his mystique, the elusive force men imagined lay behind the facade of genial composure. Old players, even the greatest of them, who shared extraordinary days and nights with Busby, remain in awe of him. They speak of always wanting to please him. Long after they were famous, universally adored and in all worldly ways secure, it was Sir Matt's attention and affection men like Bobby Charlton, Johnny Carey, Denis Law, George Best and Harry Gregg craved. Great athletes felt inadequate in his presence, although he had ostensibly done nothing to induce the feeling.

Eamon Dunphy, journalist and former United apprentice.

If Busby had stood dressed for the pit, and somebody alongside him in the room had worn ermine, there would have been no difficulty about deciding who was special. Granting him a knighthood did not elevate him. It raised, however briefly, the whole dubious phenomenon of the honours system.

Hugh McIlvanney, journalist.

They should rename Old Trafford the Matt Busby Stadium because for so many years he was Manchester United.

Tommy Docherty.

He is flawless in his dealing with us. He can remain aloof and yet human. He can tear us apart and still command respect. He can praise us, and we know it to be genuine. He can advise us and we know there is no dark motive afoot. He can talk to us and we will always listen. The manager-player relationship at Old Trafford is ideal.

George Best.

I have often been asked what made Matt Busby so special and really it was the simplest thing in the world. He treated his players like human beings!

Denis Law.

You would go in fighting and full of demands. And he would give you nothing at all. He might even take a tenner off your wages. And you would come out thinking, 'what a great guy'.
Eamon Dunphy.

In a way Matt is like a successful preacher. He makes you believe what he believes. His way of doing things, the only way of doing things. His mixture of personal humility and ruthless judgement is what makes the challenge of being a Manchester United player so exhilarating. You know you won't be judged by match results, but individually by mysterious standards buried deep inside Matt himself and only him.
Albert Quixall, the former United inside-forward.

I think he put Manchester on the map more than any other human being, not just United but Manchester itself.
Pat Crerand.

Footballers are people first, that was Busby's secret. Even the oldest men were boys to him.
Eamon Dunphy.

Matt will seek the board's advice, ponder over it and then go away and do precisely as he wants.
Harold Hardman, the former United director.

Matt was the eternal optimist. In 1968 he still hoped Glenn Miller was just missing.
Pat Crerand. *Glenn Miller was an American band leader who disappeared during WW2 while flying to entertain troops in France.*

Busby emanated presence, substance, the quality of strength without arrogance. No man in my experience ever exemplified better the ability to treat you as an equal while leaving you with the sure knowledge that you were less than he was. Such men do not have to be appointed leaders. Some democracy of the instincts and the blood elects them to be in charge.

Hugh McIlvanney.

You could easily be fooled into accepting Busby as everyone's kind uncle. That's how he comes over to the public. But he can be as practical and cunning as the best of them. As far as I am concerned he has been the greatest manager of his time and at times one of the toughest.

Maurice Setters, the former United wing-half.

Whenever Sir Matt came up and put his arm round you it invariably meant you were about to be dropped.

Denis Law.

There are people in football who will tell you that if justice were done Matt Busby would be the first knight since Sir Thomas More to be canonised. They may add, for emphasis, that More was not in the same class as a wing-half.

Hugh McIlvanney.

He has held his magnetism right through five decades. I remember in Rotterdam for the final of the Cup-Winners' Cup, a lot of fans were gathered at the main entrance chanting the names of players like 'Hughesy' as they went in in. Suddenly Sir Matt arrived and the wild cheering turned to respectful applause. It was quite touching, just like the Pope arriving.

Sir Alex Ferguson.

Matt was still struggling to recover from the injuries he received at Munich. He walked with a stick. Jimmy Murphy walked alongside, lending him a hand. In complete silence, Matt walked round our dressing room, shaking every player by the hand. He congratulated us all individually. Something – something very special – made that man come into our dressing room in what must have been one of the saddest moments of his life to congratulate us on beating his team. Tommy Banks summed it up for us all when he said,'that's the finest sportsman you'll ever see'. No wonder Matt's teams always played for him. How could you fail to respect a man like that?

Nat Lofthouse after the 1958 FA Cup final, which United lost to Bolton, a few months after the Munich tragedy.

Big talk in the dressing room was one thing, dealing with, 'the Boss' in his office was a very different experience. His presence was overwhelming. You were not confronted, on the contrary, he was charming, solicitous, understanding your concerns, keen that you should understand Manchester United's interests as well as your own. He didn't make you feel bad, he made you feel important, you wanted to please him. do what was right for everyone, yourself and the club. He was the club. You signed. And felt like a shit for causing hassle in the first place. Then you thanked him. On the way down the stairs you tried to figure out a way to explain to the others what had happened.

Eamon Dunphy.

SELF-IMAGE

There should be a plaque on the wall saying, 'the beast was born here'.

Sir Alex Ferguson on a visit in 1995 to the house he was brought up in.

It's bloody tough being a legend.

Ron Atkinson.

I'm a whole-hearted player and I can't sit back and spray 50 yard passes around, take the occasional free-kick and that's my night's work. If I don't get stuck in I usually have a bad game. Work-rate is a vital part of my game and I can't change.

Roy Keane.

Sometimes I feel like a one-man zoo.

George Best in 1973.

I'm a better ball player than George Best. George definitely had the edge over me in finishing but when it comes to beating people and creating chances for others, well, I could lose George at that.

Willie Morgan.

I'm no angel and I've had a lot of trouble.

Roy Keane.

I'm a lucky guy to be where I am today. Forget the National Lottery – I've really hit the jackpot here at Old Trafford.

Steve Bruce.

I was just one of the players who got the ball for better players to play with.

Tony Dunne, full-back in the 1960s.

I've no left foot, I'm not too good in the air and I'm not that fast. I've loads of weaknesses.

Norman Whiteside.

I've never been a unique talent. I've always been working, working my way to the top.

Teddy Sheringham.

I think the Doc bought me just to make the other players laugh.
Gordon Hill, United winger in the 1970s, on Tommy Docherty.

My settee – it's a big lolloping casual sort of thing and it's not too fancy. That just about sums me up.
Lee Sharpe.

I don't think I'm blessed with any outstanding skills, but you can guarantee that I always try to do my best. Sometimes it's not good enough, but sometimes it is
Steve Bruce.

Freedom of expression brings genius, brings euphoria, brings fire. I play with passion and fire. I have to accept that sometimes this fire does harm. I harm myself. I am aware of it. I harm others.
Eric Cantona.

Footballers are no different to a milkman or a dustman. We're just in the limelight and get paid a lot of money.
David Beckham.

You can say I'm replacing Eric [Cantona], but I don't see it that way. It's a pressure in itself joining the club so I'm not getting involved in talking about succeeding Eric.
Teddy Sheringham.

I'm an ordinary fellow. I never know what is expected of me when I'm introduced to people. If I talked a lot about myself, I'd be called bigheaded, so I say nothing. But whatever I did or said, they'd be some people who would find it wrong.
Sir Bobby Charlton.

Was I the fifth Beatle? Not really. What I think they meant was that I wasn't your average 'don't do anything until Saturday' footballer.

George Best, who was given this title by the media owing to his huge talent, enormous popularity, long-haired good looks and celebrity lifestyle.

Funny, romantic and hard.

Wayne Rooney's self image.

Just as I can bring happiness to people with my spontaneity, my instinctiveness, so there are always going to be dark shadows, black stains.

Eric Cantona.

I can't rely on my skill as there is not much there. So I really have to rely on getting stuck in.

Roy Keane.

A half-blind dwarf.

Nobby Stiles's self image.

I don't have any fancy ideas about my importance to the team. A lot of players better than I am have left and United have continued to be successful.

Roy Keane.

I was a hard worker. I knew what I could do and what I couldn't do and that was my greatest attribute as a player.

Steve Coppell.

I like to be anonymous. I'm not that interesting. Anyway, there's nothing to find out. My privacy and my family are the most important things to me. I don't have the hunger to show everybody how well-off I am.

Ole Gunnar Solskjaer.

At Leeds I had become just another cog in the machine. And deep down I am not a cog, content to play a small part in a team who run on their own power.

Eric Cantona.

I've been a bit of a poser all my life. I get some stick from the lads in the dressing room, but I can handle it.

David Beckham.

I'm lucky. I know what it's like to want things and to walk down to the shops and wish you had what's in them.

Rio Ferdinand.

I know I have never been that popular and I know that some people want to string me up.

Martin Edwards, the former chief executive and chairman.

RETIREMENT

Manchester United is a very special club. A club that I have searched for all my life but the time is right to move on.

Eric Cantona.

In life, there is nothing as intense as what you felt as a footballer and I prefer to leave it at that. In real life, what could we do together? We could meet for an evening, have a drink, speak about the past and what then? After that it becomes ordinary. It is like you have had an intense love affair with somebody and you separate. Later you can meet for a coffee, but what good does it do? You're not going to get back together and you're not going to feel like you did before.

Eric Cantona.

A footballer is like a precious flower that blossoms only for a short time, as one of our greatest contemporary philosophers might have said. In a dream, fame is sweeter than the tart flesh of apples to children. But sometimes the dream must come to an end and it is time to wake up. The poet must look out the window of the speeding train and know that his terminus is arriving. For every time there is a football season, there is a time to play and a time to go. Now it is the time to go and for the doctorates to be written.

The Independent newspaper's editorial on Eric Cantona's retirement.

I don't feel let down. This is the longest Eric has played for any club – a third of his career, which is a measure of how he regarded United. There's absolutely no recriminations on my part. At £1 million we've had unbelievable value out of him, so we wish him well. We got six trophies for that money.

Sir Alex Ferguson on Cantona's retirement.

Basically it's a case of, 'let's get on without him'. He has gone and it's not as if we're coming in here every day and saying, 'where's Eric?' It makes you think what it would be like if you left yourself – nobody would give two hoots. But then this is a club that has lost a big player every season and it was the same when Bryan Robson left, Steve Bruce, Mark Hughes, Paul Ince and Andrei Kanchelskis – and now Eric. Life goes on without him.

Gary Neville.

I don't believe in retirement. It's against the law in America to force people to retire. I still have plenty of damage to do.

Sir Alex Ferguson.

When my brother [Bobby] stopped playing they should have shot him. He was so unhappy.

Jack Charlton.

Alex Ferguson loves the game and will die on the United bench, I am sure of that.

Eric Cantona.

I hope he was talking about when I'm 92!

Sir Alex Ferguson's response.

I leave when I need to change. It's like being with a woman. If you get to the point when you've got nothing left to say to her, you leave. Or else you stop being good.

Eric Cantona.

It's difficult enough replacing him as a monument in the team without having to replace him as a person as well.

Tommy Docherty after Bobby Charlton retired.

I love this club. I know I'm making the right decision about management but I want to stay in touch with the club, to feel I'm part of United. It's not a Matt Busby situation we're talking about, it's a modern day development in football. Sixteen years here is a hell of a term. I've dealt with contracts, player agents, the media, TV, it's a completely different ball-game now. It's pressure.

Sir Alex Ferguson announcing his retirement in 2001.

When I was at St Mirren, I ran two pubs as well as managing the football team. I would drop the kids off at school in the morning and not return home until late at night. I didn't see them grow up, but I did see a lot of young footballers grow up. That is why I think they see me more as a friend than a father. That is, perhaps, one of the big reasons why I am leaving. I hope I can make up for lost time.

Sir Alex Ferguson.

I had two offers from AC Milan, but before I became famous no-one wanted me. The reason I stayed at Old Trafford is that, frankly, I didn't think it could get any better anywhere else. Leaving United is going to be very tough indeed.

Sir Alex Ferguson.

It was really Cathy's [his wife] idea. If she hadn't come up with it and the boys hadn't given full support, I wouldn't have considered a change of mind. But I do have to confess that maybe it was an idea I was hoping deep down she would come up with.

Sir Alex Ferguson after changing his mind about retiring.

From the minute I changed my mind about retiring I have got something back in myself. I have enjoyed my football this year. I started planning about Manchester United again, started thinking about the future of the club and I have enjoyed that.

Sir Alex Ferguson.

I quit the game too young [30] but I didn't have the passion to keep going to bed early, not going out with friends and not drinking.

Eric Cantona.

I am not going to leave this club in a shambles when I go. They have been too good to me for that. The manager who follows me will find that he inherits a squad in good shape, with quality players. However, that's for the future.

Sir Alex Ferguson.

Retirement is like a death. When you are a footballer, you do something very public, you do it because it is a passion and you feel alive when you're doing it. You feel alive also because people recognise you for the job you do. Then you quit and it's like a death. A lot of footballers are afraid and that is why they go on TV to speak about the game. They don't speak to teach the public or to give a point of view, they do it for themselves. It is important because it helps them to feel alive again, to deal with their fears about this death.

Eric Cantona.

Be glad when all this presentation stuff is over. Nobody's going to put me in a home, you know.

Sir Bobby Charlton after his last match for United.

You'll miss Manchester United more than they'll miss you.

Ian Rush after Cantona retired.

I am over the moon.

David Beckham after Sir Alex decided to stay at Old Trafford.

REFEREES

Can anybody tell me why they give referees a watch? It's certainly not to keep the time. I think it was a Mickey Mouse one.

Sir Alex Ferguson unhappy at referee Graham Poll's reluctance to add more than three minutes of injury time in a game with Everton.

I have to hand it to Manchester United. They have the best players – and the best referees.

Sam Hammam, then owner of Wimbledon.

In the tunnel I say to [David] Elleray, 'you might as well book me now and get it over with'. He takes it pretty well but he still books me.

Roy Keane.

I can't stand Alex Ferguson.

Dorothy Elleray, Elleray's grandmother.

That was out of order. That referee, he didn't deserve that. I shouldn't have been chasing a referee around Old Trafford and I apologised to him; well, I kind of apologised. I saw him a few months later, he was assistant ref at Leicester. I wouldn't say we had a laugh and a joke about it, but we had a good giggle. That will never happen again, honestly. No way would I go round pointing the finger ever again. Referees do a hard job and they do it very well. If our mistakes were blown out of proportion like theirs … God!

Roy Keane after he, Nicky Butt, David Beckham, Jaap Stam and Gary Neville chased referee Andy D'Urso after he awarded a penalty to Middlesbrough at Old Trafford in January, 2000.

It was my first season in the Premier League, my first time refereeing Manchester United and my first time at Old Trafford. With more experience I would have stood my ground. I kept saying, 'go away', but the further back I walked the more they walked on. A more experienced referee would not have retreated. But there are no grudges.

Andy D'Urso.

I thought our players went too far. I must say that, and I've told them so this morning. I've watched it on TV and I can understand his reasons for giving it.

Sir Alex Ferguson on the same event.

If the ref had stood still we wouldn't have had to chase him.

Roy Keane on the D'Urso incident.

It is no good being meek and mild when you are faced by a snarling Roy Keane. He is going to eat you up and spit you out in bubbles.

Jeff Winter, retired referee.

AGGRAVATION

Aggression is what I do. I go to war. You don't contest football matches in a reasonable state of mind.

Roy Keane.

You always knew when the hairdryer was coming because he grabs the cuffs on his suit.

Bryan Robson on Sir Alex Ferguson.

As soon as we started training, [Keane] put in one of those tackles. I think he was saying, 'let's see if you really want that money'.
Dwight Yorke in his early days at United.

Listen, if you ever kick my husband, I will come round and kick you. And he's all, 'nah, straight up, I love David'. And I said, 'well just you remember what I said because I will'. And I would.
What Victoria Beckham said to Dennis Wise.

I think players were aware of me because I had this reputation and that would mean they were thinking about me, especially early on in matches. That was generally a good thing, because if they were thinking about me then they weren't concentrating on their game. It was my job to intimidate players.
Nobby Stiles.

They've obviously never been to a Glasgow wedding.
Sir Alex Ferguson declaring no worries about the possible hostile atmosphere at United's Champions' league clash away to Galatasaray in the mid-nineties.

I get stick everywhere. Makes me feel at home.
Roy Keane.

Their tactics began to resemble a commando raid: knock out the main installations – which meant the key players – then get on with the job.
Denis Law on Leeds United in the 1960s and '70s.

Do they hate us? You take a corner kick at Elland Road and you've got 15,000 horrible skinheads in their end yelling murder at you.
Ryan Giggs.

At Anfield things tend to be a bit more basic. They throw 50p pieces at me, yelling abuse. I have my own way of dealing with that. I put the ball down, take one step, kick it and then run off to the safety of the penalty area, where I've only got Neil Ruddock to worry about.

Ryan Giggs.

Every team had a hard man. We had Nobby Stiles, Chelsea had Chopper [Harris], Arsenal had Peter Storey, Liverpool had Tommy Smith. Leeds had eleven of them.

George Best.

I don't really like playing against the clever ones like Gascoigne. I prefer someone like Whiteside, where you can get stuck in, get a bit back and have a good laugh about it.

Vinnie Jones.

Now listen, boys, I'm not happy with our tackling. We're hurting them, but they keep getting up.

Jimmy Murphy, the former United assistant manager.

I used to hit people over the head with my handbag if they shouted names like 'dirty Jones' when Mark committed a foul or if they threw other abuse at him when he made a mistake.

June Jones, widow of Mark Jones, who lost his life in the Munich disaster.

Nobby Stiles is a dangerous marker, tenacious and sometimes brutal. He takes recourse to anything to contain his man. Very badly intentioned. A bad sportsman.

Otto Gloria, Benfica coach, around the time of the 1968 European Cup final.

Stiles. The Assassin of Madrid.

Spanish newspaper headline after United beat Real Madrid in the semi-final of the 1968 European Cup.

Then we were laughing and I was somehow happy I'd been hit with the bottle. If we had lost they would have thrown flowers at me.

Nobby Stiles after the same game.

Sometimes players just want to kick the living daylights out of you because you are Dwight Yorke. Fair enough.

Dwight Yorke.

It was like Vietnam sometimes.

Ron Atkinson on games between Liverpool and United.

Things like that happen in the dressing room. It was one of those freak accidents of nature that happens and then it's over. What a freak, it will never happen again.

Sir Alex Ferguson, who accidentally struck David Beckham on the head after kicking a football boot across the dressing room following United's defeat by Arsenal in the 2003 FA Cup.

What happened in the United changing room has happened to me 50 times in my career. I have kicked bottles of mineral water, bags and shoes but I never hit a player. It's a question of technique, and the Scots must have a better technique.

Marcello Lippi, then Juventus coach, on the same incident.

It's the first time we've had to replace divots in the players.

Ron Atkinson after a tough game against Valencia.

When I first signed schoolboy forms for United, as a midfield player, I felt for a while that I was just treading water. There was a build-up of frustration because I felt that I wasn't showing how good I could be, so I started lashing out a bit. And when I started getting aggressive, I started making progress. So I stuck with it.

Mark Hughes.

I enjoy being put up there with the likes of Tommy Smith, Dave Mackay and Norman Hunter. They're a great set of lads. I've even worked with Tommy and Norman on the dinner circuit. We called it the hard man show.

Nobby Stiles.

When I played and a goalkeeper held the ball on the goal-line he went into the back of the net.

Jack Rowley, United striker in the 1940s and 50s.

When David Beckham was a kid at United everyone thought he was too soft to make it. We had to make him more aggressive. It was the only way he could become a top professional.

Bryan Robson.

PROBLEMS

In one of my first games at Old Trafford I had to do a man-marking job on Jimmy Greaves – my eyes were so bad I followed the wrong player around for five minutes.

Nobby Stiles, who suffered from shortsightedness early in his career.

When I came in we used to be a rollercoaster outfit. We could beat anybody, but anybody could beat us.

Sir Alex Ferguson.

We were very disappointed we couldn't play on Saturday, because like United we had supporters coming from all over the country. There were two coming from London, one from Newcastle, one from Brighton.

David Kilpatrick, Rochdale chairman, after his side's 3rd round FA Cup tie against United was postponed.

My mother always told me to look after the little one. I had to take him with me wherever I went and I moaned like hell about it. Later, when we played against each other in league football, I remember she was still telling me to lay off him. It didn't really matter because I could never catch him, even then.

Jack Charlton.

Mentally and physically I am a bloody wreck. Not eating. Not sleeping. Heavy drinking and staying out until four or five in the morning because I was frightened to go to my gold-fish bowl of a home.

George Best.

I am allergic to grass! It's why you never see me rolling around when I get injured.

Ole Gunnar Solskjaer.

If someone says to me, 'let him know that you are there', it does not mean that I should go up to my marker and say, 'good afternoon, my name is Andrei Kanchelskis and I've just arrived from Kirovograd'. It means that you have to make your presence felt.

Andrei Kanchelskis wrestling with the complexities of the English language after his arrival at Old Trafford from the Ukraine.

Genius is about digging yourself out of this big hole which you find yourself in, or in which others have put you. That's genius.

Eric Cantona.

It went through my mind to go abroad because people were saying that I would not be able to go to certain grounds. I was a 22-year-old boy wanting to play football for a team I love, but at times I feared for my safety. There were so many threats that were coming through, not just to me but to my whole family. That was hard, but one of the first people to call me was Alex Ferguson. He said, 'don't worry son, get yourself back to Manchester and to the people that love you and you'll be fine'.

David Beckham on his difficulties at the 1998 World Cup.

I realise it's very important for the country. I don't know enough about stress fractures. But I do know he is not doing the right things to get it fixed.

The Queen on David Beckham's broken foot before the 2002 World Cup.

Nothing is more important to England's arrangements for the World Cup than the state of David Beckham's foot.

Tony Blair, prime minister, on the same injury.

I couldn't believe what we woke up to. What was my foot doing on the front page of the newspapers?!

David Beckham.

PRESSURE

Fergie, Fergie, on the dole.

Supporters' chant after United lost 3-0 to Aston Villa in 1989.

Fergie Out!

The first front cover headline in Red Issue, the United fanzine, which appeared in February 1989.

Three years of excuses: ta ta Fergie.

Banner held aloft by United fans after Sir Alex Ferguson had been manager for three years.

I used to look at Gordon McQueen, who would throw up on the pitch actually before the kick-off with nerves and I knew how he felt. I used to relish matches away from Old Trafford. My record was actually pretty good – 25 games, 12 goals – but most of the goals were away from home, which is crazy.

Alan Brazil, United striker in the 1980s.

I'm careful of the players I lay into. Some can't handle it. Some can't even handle a team talk. There are some I don't look in the eye during a team talk because I know I'm putting them under pressure.

Sir Alex Ferguson

The singular fact that drives us Scots is fear of failure and a compelling determination to succeed. We cross the border into England to prove ourselves

Sir Alex Ferguson.

It's great to be on the pitch, that's when you feel the least pressure.

Roy Keane.

It's pressure that makes the game beautiful.

Eric Cantona.

I don't know what stress or pressure is. I don't understand these things.

Dwight Yorke.

Alex is a canny old Scot, all right. He knows all about playing mind games. He's putting out the bowl of milk for us but we're not going to lap it up. He's a master at psyching people out. But psychology won't work on us. We've got too many psychos in the squad.

Joe Kinnear, then Wimbledon boss, after praise from Sir Alex Ferguson.

I don't lose sleep over our troubles. I went through the insomnia thing years ago when I was at Weymouth and we were near the bottom of the Southern League.

Frank O'Farrell.

I don't have many regrets. If there is one big one it is leaving United as early as I did because I could have become a multi-millionaire. Too bad, but at the time I just couldn't handle it. The pressure was too much for me.

George Best.

You feel you have to be brilliant all the time.

David Beckham.

Pressure for me is growing up in poverty. Not having shoes on your feet and no money in your pocket. Now that's pressure. And that's exactly what I experienced as a youngster in Tobago. Now my life has changed completely.

Dwight Yorke.

I couldn't handle the pressure – 60,000 at Old Trafford is a lot of people to please – and because, as a United player, your life's not your own. I'd open a bottle of wine on a Friday night and sit up drinking until three in the morning to calm my nerves for next day's match. It helped me relax and get to sleep but didn't affect my performance as I was so fit.

Mickey Thomas, United winger in the 1980s.

They tell me to do so many things, so many bloody things: shave off my beard, cut my hair – as if that would make me into what they wanted me to be. Jesus Christ had a beard and long hair and they didn't want to change him.

George Best

We were having a really bad time, near the bottom of the league and we, the players, were being criticised every Sunday and Monday. That was it but the manager was getting it every day and he never once came in and said, 'you're the reason for this'. He carried the burden himself.

Brian McClair on Sir Alex Ferguson

I can't explain what has gone wrong. But it is with me all the time, even when I try to sleep. And the more I think about it, the harder it becomes.

Diego Forlan, who took 27 games to score his first goal for United.

When you're from Manchester, the crowd knows that your heart is fully in it and they can go easy on you … but it makes no odds with the manager – if you play a bad pass, it doesn't matter where you come from, you'll get a roasting.

Nicky Butt.

Today these athletes face so many more demands. The old footballer, who was all muscle or all talent, would be overwhelmed. As soon as you step off the pitch, you have a microphone shoved under your nose even on it, if the match is live on TV in certain countries. Footballers today have to know how to think, speak, act and know what to say and what not to say. Otherwise they are finished. Today's footballers need to be perfect in almost every way. They need to be colder and more detached, because they are obliged to be less vulnerable.

Sir Alex Ferguson.

I felt like putting my head in the gas oven and I know there'd be 20,000 people queuing up to turn on the taps for me.

Sir Alex Ferguson in 1990.

Having managed United, I'm aware of the expectancy there but there's a need to deliver at every club. If I hadn't won promotion at Cambridge, or at least been in the race, I'd have been looking over my shoulder. I can honestly say I didn't feel any greater pressure at Old Trafford than anywhere else.

Ron Atkinson.

I don't know how many managers have lost their jobs this season but I know all of us have faced anxiety at one stage or another. But if you put us all together I doubt whether the pressure would match up to what Alex [Ferguson] has faced.

Brian Clough speaking in 1990.

OOPS!

Tell Alex Ferguson we're coming to get him.

Kevin Keegan after Newcastle United won promotion to the Premiership in the early 1990s.

You don't win anything with kids.

Alan Hansen in 1995, when United started the season with a very young team and lost their first game, but went on to win the Premiership.

I am hurt and upset by what is happening. Alex is destroying United. We'd love to praise Alex. But what has he given us in over 3 years?

Tommy Docherty in 1990.

It will need an awful lot of bad luck for my team to return home defeated. If this does happen, then it will demonstrate that football follows an inhuman logic.

Mario Coluna, the Benfica captain, before the 1968 European Cup final.

My conviction that by the time I retire I will have won all the major prizes the game has to offer has never wavered.

Ron Atkinson.

United's participation was not in the best interests of the League.

The Football League on United's early European games.

People hate Manchester United because they are so successful. People will hate us in a few years because we will be winning everything.

Jonathan Woodgate, Leeds United defender.

Eric Cantona was sold to Manchester United because of a vision I couldn't get out of my mind. It kept repeating itself – the sight of the Frenchman disappearing over the horizon astride his Harley-Davidson with paint brushes and easel strapped on his back. It is an illusion that might yet come to haunt Alex Ferguson at Old Trafford.

Howard Wilkinson, then Leeds United boss, after he sold Cantona to United.

I've had my ups and downs with Alex [Ferguson], but I do believe that overall he's been a fine boss at Old Trafford. I know he'll be haunted by the ghost of Mark Robins, the lad he let go to shoot Norwich to the top of the Premier League.

Tommy Docherty.

They're waiting to crown new kings out there. Get out and take the chance.

Frank O'Farrell to Ted MacDougall as he made his debut for United.

They are just another English club. It doesn't make any difference if we are playing Sheffield United or Manchester United. All English teams play the same way.

Ronald Koeman, the Barcelona sweeper, before the European Cup Winner's Cup final against United in 1991.

If he ever makes a First Division footballer, I'm Mao Tse-tung.

Tommy Docherty on Dwight Yorke.

My favourite Manchester United player is Michael Owen.

Pele.

Fergie OBE – Out Before Easter.

Emlyn Hughes in 1989 when Sir Alex Ferguson was struggling.

Cristiano Ronaldo is a puffball who's never done it on a big occasion … I don't think they'll do it tonight because they're playing against good, experienced professionals. Maybe I'll have an egg on my face in a few hours' time, but I doubt it.

Eamon Dunphy, journalist and former United youth player, before United beat Roma 7-1 in the Champions' League. Ronaldo scored twice.

He has become the Margaret Thatcher of football, a once omnipotent leader clinging to office long after his powers have waned, while other, lesser figures try to summon the courage to make the first stab in the back.

David Thomas, Daily Mail columnist, after Sir Alex Ferguson ended the2004/05 season empty-handed.

There are two professional teams from London – Manchester United and Chelsea and they are both awesome.

P. Diddy, rapper.

I want to build an empire here like Alex Ferguson has done at Old Trafford.

David O'Leary when boss of Leeds United.

It's a panic buy.

Emlyn Hughes after United signed Eric Cantona.

Oh, Teddy, Teddy, went to Man United and you won f*** all.

Opposing fans' chant aimed at Teddy Sheringham before he won the Treble.

I definitely want Brooklyn to be christened, but I don't know into what religion yet.

David Beckham.

Getting lost in Liverpool taught me a very early lesson to leave my car in France and use taxis in future in this country. It's hard enough learning a new language and everything new on top of that – but you even drive on the left-hand side of the road here as well. I'm still trying to live down getting lost in Liverpool for two hours. Whenever I asked for directions, people killed themselves with laughter.

Fabien Barthez.

I have disconnected myself from West Ham and signed a contract with Liverpool. I can consider myself a Red Devil.

Javier Mascherano, after signing for Liverpool.

My son will not go to Chelsea. Over my dead body will he go there. They have an owner who has no philosophy or structure at the club. Chelsea just buy expensive players all over Europe and think it will make them a great team. But my son has been to see Sir Alex Ferguson and nobody knows better why organisation and a good structure at a top club is so important. Old Trafford is the only place he wants to play and if he can't play there he would rather stay at PSV. In fact he would rather play in their reserves than go to Chelsea. It's as simple as that.

Arjen Robben's dad.

I want our fans to be happy and for them to enjoy the experience of being at Old Trafford. I would appeal to them to just enjoy the performance we intend to put on for them.

Roma's Francesco Totti before United won 7-1 in the Champions' League.

It is an increasingly inescapable conclusion that, unwittingly or otherwise, Ferguson is winding down, a prize-fighter who no longer has the stomach or the wit for an admittedly enormous challenge which, once upon a time, he would have fervently inhaled.

Rob Smyth, journalist, in July 2006.

MONEY

Money in the bank is no use to a football team. You have to put your money on the field where the public can see it.

Sir Matt Busby.

Money has not been my motive. I think I'm sentimental about football. I would rather tell my children about the medals I've won and the goals I scored than how much I earned.

Sir Bobby Charlton.

United were bad payers in the 1970s. I think they had the mentality that footballers would play for them for nothing. People moan about agents but I wish they'd been around in my day.

Stuart Pearson, striker in the 1970s.

I spent a lot of money on booze, birds and fast cars. The rest I just squandered.

George Best.

The stadium has certainly changed a lot since my day and they never had raffles to give away £4,000 when I was a player up there. We could only dream about being paid that much in my day.

Lou Macari.

Today's players would leave us for dead. They deserve whatever money they get.

Johnny Carey, United captain in the 1940s and '50s.

If I really like a pair of trousers there's no limit to the price I'll pay.

David Beckham.

I was probably earning £5,000 a week, but I was spending £8,000.

George Best.

People talk about the money we earn, but when we won the European Cup you could have given us anything and we wouldn't have swapped it for that moment.

Denis Irwin after winning the Champions' League.

My love for United is greater than my need for more money.

Ole Gunnar Solskjaer.

If Roy Keane earns four or five times what I do, he deserves that. He's more important than me.

Gary Neville after Roy Keane signed a contract worth an estimated £52,000 per week.

If you play in the first team at United, your wages are astronomical. Honestly, what we earn is not just a whacking amount of money by Dutch standards, it's obscene when you compare it to what is earned in the rest of Europe. As a player you choose a club and you pick the ideal country where you want to play, but I admit that the size of your wage packet plays a major part.

Ruud van Nistelrooy.

The average working lad can't understand or relate to the money in the game, but he'll go along with it if he believes it will make his team better.

Sir Alex Ferguson.

The salaries players get, I don't think can ever be a good thing for the game. You think to yourself, 'how's it come to this?'. The modern man has changed. There's a need to be recognised, a need to be known. You see that with earrings, tattoos, the way that dress sense and hairstyles change every six months.

Sir Alex Ferguson.

During the excitement I lost a £1,000 cheque that I had been given for being the Manager of the Year.

Sir Matt Busby recalling the 1968 European Cup final.

This was a bad public relations exercise and something that should never have happened. I'm still waiting for my apology.

Roy Keane after United sent a letter to season ticket holders blaming Keane's increase in salary for the increase in ticket prices.

I never played for money. If I had never been paid, I would still have played with the same passion.

Eric Cantona.

It's just the image rights that needed a little perking

David Beckham on delays in signing a contract at United.

There is a shopping mall in Holland which is for sale for 31 million guilders, so I was worth four million guilders more than the mall!

Jaap Stam on his £10.75 million transfer fee.

Some folks tell me that we professional players are soccer slaves. Well, if this is slavery, give me a life sentence.

Sir Bobby Charlton before the abolition of the maximum wage in 1961.

MEDIA

Criticism does not bother me. I don't read newspapers or watch sports programmes on TV. Lately I've been busy watching Teletubbies.

Juan Veron.

I've read a lot of Socrates on page three of The Sun.

Eric Cantona, on the philosopher.

It gets a bit worn out this hairdryer stuff, but in dealing with the myth you've got to deal with a lot of things. For instance, one of the broadsheets wrote that I used to go by the stand and practise screaming.

Sir Alex Ferguson.

I was God's gift to the press, wasn't I? I used to start sounding off and they'd say,'hold on Tom, we can't get it all down'. So I'd say the same outrageous things, only slower.
Tommy Docherty.

I think I have already doubled the number of interviews I've ever done in the last couple of weeks. I never used to think I had anything interesting to say, but if I'm captain of Manchester United I must have, mustn't I?
Roy Keane.

When I look at the way United protect Ryan Giggs from the media and everything else, I wonder if that might have helped. There is a lot of advice for stars like Ryan, but I don't know. If they had told me how to behave I would probably have done the opposite.
George Best.

A lot of the lads tell me when they're on holiday they spend their time on the beach reading about me.
Ryan Giggs.

I don't want to be on the front pages. I want to be on the back.
David Beckham.

Everyone makes mistakes – mine just seem to get more publicity than other people's.
George Best.

They don't get read in my house. That's just the way I am. Apart from rare praise, I know what they are going to say about me beforehand. I don't need them to rub my nose in it. I just don't talk to them, so they write what they want anyway.
Andy Cole on newspapers.

When I quit playing a tabloid newspaper offered me a lot of money – in excess of £25,000 – to slag off Fergie. I turned it down. I'm not the sort of guy to do that and, anyway, I have nothing against him. We always got on well and when United won the title he invited me into his office to join his family celebration. He must have known that meant sending out for an extra case of champagne.

Norman Whiteside.

There is no doubt that much of the bile directed at David Beckham at football grounds is created by the kind of journalism that is at best mischievous and at worse malignant. It is the kind of propaganda that leads to nutters trying to snatch their child, kidnap threats on an almost daily basis, abusive and pornographic mail. It is hatred normally reserved for paedophiles and rapists and it is directed towards a footballer, a pop singer and their 18-month-old child.

Michael Parkinson.

The media has changed enormously. There are so many papers, so many TV stations. The interest in football has grown phenomenally. A guy like me is on the back pages every day and gets a microphone shoved under his nose even before he has left the pitch. There is always a headline that judges you, whether you are innocent or guilty. It is very difficult to live like this. Eventually it wears you down. I have been doing it for a very long time – 15 years at United alone.

Sir Alex Ferguson.

Stop reading the papers.

Sir Matt Busby's advice to Sir Alex Ferguson when he was under pressure.

I've never enjoyed doing interviews. I always run out of the back door of the training ground to avoid the press. I jump into my car and drive off, leaving it to the others.

Paul Scholes.

Do you know that the most perfect English in the world is spoken in Scotland? That's absolutely correct by the way. If you go up to Inverness for a day you will learn how to speak English perfectly.

Sir Alex Ferguson to a South Korean journalist.

I might go to Alcoholics Anonymous but I think it would be difficult for me to remain anonymous.

George Best.

MANAGING

I'm not here to please the players. They are here to please me.

Sir Alex Ferguson.

That's what the manager does. He gives you confidence, but he doesn't give you too much of it.

David Beckham.

Control is everything in management. Unless you have control, you can't have a vision, targets, dreams. In football life, the only thing that gives you control is time and the only thing that buys you time is success.

Sir Alex Ferguson.

You can have my home number, but please remember not to call during The Sweeney.

Ron Atkinson to journalists after he was appointed boss of United.

No, I am not a Catholic – but I'm willing to be converted.

Ron Atkinson, the first non-Roman Catholic manager at United for over 30 years, after his appointment.

He came a stranger and left a stranger.

Denis Law on Frank O'Farrell.

I gave the club the FA Cup. They gave me the sack.

Tommy Docherty, who was sacked shortly after winning the 1977 FA Cup.

Came as a boy and left as an old man.

Tony Dunne on Wilf McGuinness.

I have been punished for falling in love.

Tommy Docherty, who was sacked for his affair with the wife of the club physiotherapist. They lived happily ever after.

The thing that got him sacked wasn't the falling in love – it was making the physio reserve team manager, sending him on scouting trips and giving his wife one while he was away.

Willie Morgan on Tommy Docherty's sacking.

I always felt that my destiny lay at Old Trafford. Now the chance to manage the biggest club in British football was there for the taking. I didn't need a second prompting. I told the United directors I would walk from Scotland to Old Trafford for the job.

Tommy Docherty.

One man stopped me winning the championship for Manchester United. Not once, but three times. His name: Ian Rush.

Ron Atkinson.

Jock Stein once told me that he turned down the job with United and he regretted it all his life. I am determined not to miss the chance. I feel dreadful about leaving Aberdeen after such a marvellous time with them.

Sir Alex Ferguson.

It still hurts deep down and the anguish of losing this job won't disappear in a long time.

Ron Atkinson.

It was easier for the board of directors to sack the manager than 20 players. And it is the players who must shoulder some of the responsibility for the boss going.

Jesper Olsen after Ron Atkinson was sacked.

Win, lose or draw, this is better than working down the pit.

Sir Matt Busby.

It was afterwards that I realised how much bigger the job was than I'd thought. Only when you are outside do you see that everyone is talking about Manchester United more than any other club. You think, 'my God, were they doing that when I was here?'

Wilf McGuinness.

When I was offered the job I was both thrilled and flattered, but I could not help feeling that Manchester United and Ron Atkinson were made for each other.

Ron Atkinson.

A death by a thousand cuts.

Frank O'Farrell, describing his treatment as manager at Old Trafford.

"Right, Ron, now what kind of car were you thinking of driving?"

"Well Mr. Chairman, at West Bromwich I had a Mercedes 450sl and I was very impressed with the comfort and reliability."

"Dave Sexton had a Rover."

"Mr. Chairman, I have a dog called Charlie but I thought we were talking about motorcars not dogs."

A conversation between United's chairman Martin Edwards and Ron Atkinson during contract negotiations as he moved to the club.

The sacking of Ron Atkinson is the best thing that could happen to Manchester United and it didn't come a day too soon. I don't like to see any manager get the sack, but I can't say I feel sorry because I hate the man. His downfall has been all his own doing. I dislike him because of his flash personality.

Tommy Docherty.

Look, I left Bobby Charlton out of the side. Fair enough, I expected some reaction with a player as popular as Bobby involved. But the letters I got. They came from all over the world. And all telling me I was wrong. That's when you realise how many people are looking at you when you get a reaction like that.

Frank O'Farrell.

Frank O'Failure

Newspaper headline.

Not everyone, sadly, would play for Wilf. The side as a whole did not give a one hundred per cent effort for him. As soon as Sir Matt returned to the scene it changed at once.

David Sadler on Wilf McGuinness.

Being the flamboyant character that he is didn't really suit the Manchester public, the people on the terraces who are basically working-class. To them there was always the belief that Ron Atkinson was a big-headed bastard. He was flash and they didn't enjoy that.

Noel Cantwell, the former United captain.

There can be few managers who have lost their job after seven consecutive victories.

Dave Sexton after he was sacked as boss of United.

After becoming a cardinal in this cathedral who could go back to being a parish priest?

Tommy Docherty.

Sir Matt made this club – the tradition, the standard, the romance. All I'm trying to do is live by that. The one thing you should never do is copy or compare yourself with Sir Matt.

Sir Alex Ferguson.

I have had players who have said 'I will never become a manager'. Then they do. They get to the end of their careers and the bug gets at them. They want to stay in the game. That is what creates the insanity among them all.

Sir Alex Ferguson.

I have easily managed to escape football now for five years. I have reinvented myself, in fact. Ten years ago, after certain matches, I finished as though in a coma, harassed by my surroundings, nothing but football all the time.

Sir Alex Ferguson.

If ever a man was tailor-made to be manager of Manchester United it was Tommy Docherty, and it was though all his earlier years of management in the game had been spent preparing for this one particular job.

Steve Coppell.

You can't go into a club and tell people their fitness is terrible, that they're bevvying, they're playing too much golf and their ground is filthy. You simply have to improve things bit by bit.

Sir Alex Ferguson.

The manager of Stringfellows.

George Best when asked"who is your favourite manager?"

If someone argues with me I have to win the argument. So I start heading towards them, that's when the hairdryer comes in. I can't lose an argument. The manager can never lose an argument.

Sir Alex Ferguson.

I would only take over England if I could sabotage their team.

Sir Alex Ferguson.

When the television people asked me to play a football manager in a film, I asked how long it would take. They said about ten days and I said, 'about par for the course'.

Tommy Docherty.

The team is playing so well, I'm having to find new ways of losing my temper.

Sir Alex Ferguson.

I think Sven Eriksson would have been a nice easy choice for the United board in terms of nothing really happens, does it? He doesn't change anything. He sails along, nobody falls out with him. He comes out and says, 'the first half we were good, second half we were not so good. I am very pleased with the result'. I think he'd have been all right for United, you know what I mean? The acceptable face.

Sir Alex Ferguson on rumours that he would be replaced by Sven-Goran Eriksson after retiring.

They say management is all about making decisions and it took me just four months to decide I wasn't cut out for it.

Martin Buchan, who managed Burnley after he retired.

I don't go out of my way to prove to people who is the manager, but from time to time somebody in my job is confronted with a situation which must be handled in a manner that signifies control.

Sir Alex Ferguson.

People say that great players seldom make great managers. But that won't be a problem for me. I was never a great player. You can throw that out of the window.

Roy Keane.

The one thing I really know about Frank O'Farrell is that he was a cautious, negative manager, who indoctrinated us all with tactics.

Denis Law after O'Farrell was sacked.

The Doc's character was reflected in his team. It was harum-scarum, a bit unpredictable.

Lou Macari on Tommy Docherty.

I know people think I have indulged Eric. That's absolute nonsense. These are emotional people in emotional situations and we handle it as best we can. Eric is an emotional man. We try to guard him and warn him, but in certain situations his emotions can't be controlled.

Sir Alex Ferguson.

A lot of people there are as good as gold and the spectators are too, but it's the legend, it's what has gone before.

Dave Sexton reflects on his time at United.

United's list of signings from our City Ground reads like a Who's Who. Perhaps United haven't signed the one who could have sorted them out once and for all. I'm referring to Old Big Head here. I'm long in the tooth. I've got middle-age spread and, quite frankly, one way or another I've shot it now. But if someone at Old Trafford had the courage, conviction or whatever it needed over the years to say, ' let's go and get Cloughie' who knows what might have happened?

Brian Clough.

I probably have a ruthless streak. My loyalty is always to my players. I will do anything for them like picking them up at five o'clock in the morning if they need a lift. But when I'm selecting the team my loyalty is to the club.

Sir Alex Ferguson.

I would never have them call me, 'Sir' – it will still be, 'Boss'

Sir Alex Ferguson after receiving his knighthood.

I'm not concerned about power. But I am concerned about control. I have to make sure the boat stays on an even keel and doesn't start rocking and listing.

Sir Alex Ferguson.

He's such a good-looking bastard he makes most of us look like Béla Lugosi

Sir Alex Ferguson on Italian coach Marcello Lippi. *Béla Lugosi was an actor best known for his portrayal of Dracula in the American Broadway stage production, and subsequent film.*

I am not unmindful that my name may be associated with the failure of several of the newer members of the club to sustain the high reputations they had previously gained in first-class football; and solely with a view to relieving the executive of the club from embarrassment I have decided to place the resignation of the secretaryship in the hands of the members of the board.

James West resigning as manager in September 1903.

I've had to swap my Merc for a BMW, I'm down to my last 37 suits and I'm drinking non-vintage champagne.

Ron Atkinson after being sacked.

It will be all downhill for him from now on. Leaving Manchester United is like leaving the Hilton and booking in at some run-down little hotel round the corner.

Tommy Docherty after Ron Atkinson was sacked.

I don't get paid to panic. We have had plenty of stuttering starts. My greatest challenge is not what's happening at the moment, my greatest challenge was knocking Liverpool right off their f***ing perch. And you can print that.

Sir Alex Ferguson.

It is a tragedy that his good points are always overshadowed by his wild inconsistencies and that part of his nature which always seems to lead him into battles with other people.

Alex Stepney on Tommy Docherty

FANS

Perhaps the greatest nights of all for United supporters were the two floodlit FA Cup games with Sheffield Wednesday and West Bromwich after Munich. Then, roaring crowds of over 60,000 willed United to victory after one of the greatest exhibitions of mass encouragement ever known in Manchester's soccer history.

Peter Morris, journalist.

I took my little nephew to Old Trafford recently, he is only four and already has all the United gear, but being his first time at a live game and just seeing his face, I thought what a great thing that on a Saturday, for the rest of his life, whatever he decides to do, that he can go to relax and enjoy this amazing spectacle in this particular stadium.

Jonathan Morris, actor.

At Liverpool, fans asked for Ryan Gigg's and Lee Sharpe's autographs. When they got them they ripped them up in front of their faces. I've often asked, 'why does everyone hate us?'

Sir Alex Ferguson.

My mum's cooking pork chops on Wednesday – would you like to come round for tea?

Part of a fan's letter to Lee Sharpe.

I'm a Red! I'm mates with [Alan] Smithy, so he's my favourite player but Ronaldo doesn't suck either, he's awesome. I really like Rooney, too.

Justin Timberlake.

Eric [Cantona] signed my book, used my pen to sign everyone else's and then walked off with it. I prefer Ryan Giggs anyway.

Marie Hassell, 13, fan.

You care, care about the people who support you. At Manchester United you become one of them, you think like a supporter, suffer like a supporter.

Sir Alex Ferguson.

There's something about Cantona which symbolises what the hard-core United fan feels about themselves. Like him, we're picked on and hated because we reckon we are the best. What he was saying with that kick was what we want to say, 'you cannot say that sort of thing to us and get away with it. We are United, respect us'.

Jim White, journalist and United fan, after Cantona's kung-fu incident.

Tell the families it's nothing like Midnight Express.

A United fan who was held in jail in Turkey after United's match against Galatasaray in 1993.

If you can get us to the [FA CUP] final again next year, you can have my wife, too.

A fan to Tommy Docherty after it was revealed he was having an affair with the wife of United's physiotherapist.

Every Friday night – that is whenever Manchester United are playing at home on the following afternoon – the boat is crammed with scarf-drenched Red Devils travelling to Old Trafford to pay homage. The only other occasion on which an Irish expedition on this scale is undertaken regularly is a pilgrimage to Lourdes. For them football represents one side of religion.

John Edwards, journalist.

I'm getting a right ribbing. It's embarrassing.

United fan Todd McIlwain, who named his baby son Sparky after Mark Hughes – two days before Hughes signed for Chelsea.

You can keep your trendy bistros on the King's Road, the smell of fish andchips mingled with success down Sir Matt Busby Way will sit nicely in my nostrils.

Peter Blythe, fan.

Eric is an idol
Eric is a star
If my mother had her way
He'd also be my Pa.

Poem by 13-year-old fan Sebastian Pennells and his single-parent mum.

The growing number of hospitality packages has brought in a different type of audience. They sit and admire the ground and can't wait to be entertained, just as if they were at a theatre or musical.

Sir Alex Ferguson.

Our fans away from home are as good as any but at home you sometimes must wonder do they understand the game of football? One or two stray passes here and there and they are on players' backs and it's not on. Some people come here to Old Trafford and I don't think they can spell football never mind understand it. At the end of the day you need to get behind the team.

Roy Keane.

When I watch a game like Manchester United versus Real Madrid and Ronaldo comes off, and everybody inside Old Trafford is applauding him, even the Manchester United supporters, I say to myself, 'this is football.' It wouldn't happen in France or Spain. In Paris if you play badly they break your car. They think that'll make you play better the next day.

Nicolas Anelka after Ronaldo scored a hat-trick for Real Madrid at Old Trafford in the Champions' League.

I could cry talking about it. It was and remains the defining moment of my life. I'd followed them for so long, through their most difficult times, when I felt I was their only real supporter. I felt their pain and they felt mine. I forgave them for failing and hoped they'd forgive me for doubting them. It's such a total love affair. It's like the unconditional love you have for a child. This was a moment of sheer euphoria, followed very quickly by the thought, 'what am I going to do with the rest of my life?'

James Nesbitt, actor, after watching United win the Champions' League in 1999.

I could almost have accepted it if he'd had another woman – but to lose your husband to a bunch of footballers is a joke.

Emma Morgan, who cited her husband Kevin's fixation with United in their divorce.

A quarter of a hour with supporters now and then is the least I can give them. In France I have often refused to sign autographs and I have gone so far as to criticise the public violently. There's no love there. No passion.

Eric Cantona.

Away from home our fans are fantastic, what I'd call the hardcore fans. But at home they have a few drinks and some prawn sandwiches but they don't realise what is going on out on the pitch.

Roy Keane.

I have a prawn sandwich every now and then myself. Very rarely, mind.

Roy Keane.

It hurts when your own fans boo you; it's shattering, almost.

Rio Ferdinand.

Abroad, the crowd is too far from the players. Here the game is warmer. There is even room for love between the crowds and players. The crowd vibrates with the game.

Eric Cantona.

Pack up your Treble in your old kit bag.

Supporter's banner at the 1977 FA Cup final when Liverpool were going for the Treble of the League, the FA Cup and the European Cup. United won and Liverpool failed in their bid to win the Treble.

Cantona rules the Evans.

Banner at the 1996 FA Cup final in which Cantona scored the only goal of the game against Liverpool, who were managed by Roy Evans.

Yes we won the double last year, but now we have to go one better and do something in Europe. It's for the fans to look back and boast about the latest victory, to go into work and have a go at other fans and feel proud.

Gary Neville.

"But Daddy, that goal was offside."
"*Yes, by a mile.*"
"Surely they'll replay the game?"
"*No, they won't.*"
"But that's not fair."
"*That's football, son.*"

Conversation between United fanatic Daniel Norcross and his father after the 1976 FA Cup final when Southampton beat United 1-0.

I couldn't live without the club. I just love the thrill of match day. I used to save my dole money to cheer them on from the Stretford End. I watch them from the VIP area now but the passion is always the same.

Mick Hucknall of Simply Red.

Football feeds the soul. United has fed mine a damn sight more than acting ever will. Acting has never been my dream. I'd give it up tomorrow to play just once for United. I can unravel layers and layers of memories which all seem to go back to the game.

James Nesbitt.

There have been so many fans coming up to me and thanking me for that goal. In my mind, I'm the one who should be thanking them because I have a fantastic rapport with the fans.

Ole Gunnar Solskjaer, who scored the winner in the 1999 Champions' League final.

Someone said to me, with all these morning kick-offs, do you think they will fill Old Trafford? If it was 4 am they would still fill it.

Jimmy Armfield, broadcaster and former England defender.

Our fans are so polite. If I go out for dinner, they leave me in peace until I have finished my meal. Only when I have paid the bill do they ask me for a signature. I enjoy it that I have the chance to go out to restaurants, to the local pub in Bowden and to the cinema, without getting mobbed. The only problem I have is going shopping in Manchester. That is really impossible. That's why I don't go anymore.

Ruud van Nistelrooy.

Personally, I rate that night at Old Trafford as one of the best games in my career ... To leave the field to a standing ovation from your opponents' supporters, this is such a rare thing. For me it remains a very beautiful, very special moment

Ronaldo.

Simply Red.

The name United fanatic Mick Hucknall gave to his band.

It's hard to come across fans like that. Truly. First, how they support their own team. But then they are also so generous in recognising the merits of their rivals. I saw not only the entire stadium but also the chairman, Martin Edwards, and his board of directors, applauding Ronaldo off the pitch. In the same way that Ronaldo said afterwards he would never forget it, I won't either. That's the kind of thing that encourages you to keep going in football, because football is rivalry, it's passion, but it's also about the exaltation of those great human values the game brings out in people.

Florentino Perez, Real Madrid president, on the same game.

United have been an obsession with me since the FA Cup final success against Leicester in 1963 and the golden days of Best, Law and Charlton. They were the team to watch. My dad took me to White Hart Lane to watch them against Tottenham and they closed the turnstiles with us two paces away. It took months for me to get over that.

Angus Deayton, TV personality.

I have been amazed by the hatred shown by some of the opposing fans towards Manchester United. I have gone home from games sometimes and wondered why I bothered. We have been kicked when trying to get on the coach and I have lost count of how many times I have been spat at.

Peter Schmeichel.

The popularity of Manchester in Asia is unbelievable. People were hysterical when they saw us. Every time one of us tried to go out, everybody knew it five minutes later. Bigger than Madonna or Michael Jackson, unbelievable! Everybody had his own bodyguard, especially in Thailand. And Becks! He just couldn't move.

Mikael Silvestre.

Because of brainwashing from my daughter, I am now a United fan.

Marlene Dietrich, actress and singer, in 1965.

Supporting Manchester United will become a criminal offence for anyone born south of Crewe.

Part of the Monster Raving Looney Party's election manifesto in 2001.

The only sanctity we've got, and the only protection we've got, is from the supporters. The media aren't going to help us, so therefore we have to rely on the supporters to get us through hard times.

Sir Alex Ferguson.

Some of the supporters have been disappointed with my behaviour and have written to me about it. It doesn't surprise me that fans have sent me letters saying they are disappointed. They are entitled to their opinion. These are fans who have been supporting the club for 20 or 30 years and they felt I had gone too far. It hurts me to read that, of course. You don't just throw those letters in the bin and think nothing of it. I can get 20 good letters and then you remember the bad one. But that's a good thing.

Roy Keane on his discipline.

United fans appreciated it if you had a go. They don't like prima donnas; regardless of skill, they want to see commitment and effort. I'd have a bad game but as long as I tried the crowd were alright. But if you appeared big time, then they would dig you out. Old Trafford could be a harsh environment. And to score a goal at the Stretford End, to see all those people so happy because of something you've done was truly special. I can fully understand sportsmen who feel a hole in their lives once they have finished playing, especially those who've played for United.

Steve Coppell.

Even the teachers had to have their affiliations. In fact, I used to sometimes wonder if they had to state their allegiance on their contracts when they came into the district.

Nobby Stiles.

I think probably 99 per cent of fans know me and trust me. They know I'm always going to do my best. I've always regarded them as part of Manchester United strongly and I've always looked upon them as that extra weapon when we've needed them. They've been fantastic. I've got to know so many of them over the years on personal terms and it makes it a little bit special when you know people personally because I know how much it means to them. I can think of them at this moment in time and say how pleased I am for them.

Sir Alex Ferguson after winning the 2003 Premiership.

I want to carry on playing as long as I can and win more trophies, simple as that. But when I do hang up my boots, I'll come to watch the matches. I've got season tickets that my mum, dad, sister and granddad use to sit in the same seats every week, and I'll use those tickets for the rest of my life. I've grown up a fan and all my mates are fans and to be able to watch United with my mates will be a fantastic experience. I know it will never replace what I'm doing now, but I also know I'll always follow Manchester United.

Gary Neville.

Sir Alex, you've done so much for us and this club that even if we don't win a single trophy from now until the day you retire we should still be bowing down to you on our hands and knees to show our gratitude.

Eddie Taylor, a fan/shareholder at the United AGM in 2002.

I apologise, they didn't deserve that. In my 18 years at this club, that was the worst performance we have ever produced in the FA Cup.

Sir Alex Ferguson apologises to the fans after the 0-0 draw with Exeter.

It's the next best thing to playing. I hope I've got a few more years left in me yet because this is a dream job.

Darren Liberman, alias Fred the Red, the United mascot.

FAME

At home things are hard. For instance, my curtains are never open, I get no privacy at all. In fact, I can't remember the last time I saw daylight in my house.

David Beckham.

Nothing could have prepared me for the limelight I was thrust into at 17. I was in newspapers, magazines, on TV, and everyone in the street knew me. It was strange for me and I dealt with it by trying not to create a fuss. I've just tried to keep it that way ever since. I was never perfect by any means. I had a lot of fun and didn't always do the right things where diet, alcohol and the rest were concerned when I was 19, 20 and 21. But they were different times. We didn't know then what we do now. I wish I had done. Then again maybe I don't, because I had some great life experiences as a youngster.

Ryan Giggs.

One day I'd like to be as charismatic as him.

David Beckham on Eric Cantona.

I can't understand the fascination there is surrounding my every move. It does get on top of me and I have to shut myself off. I go for drives in the middle of the night to be alone and I enjoy cooking for myself at home. It takes my mind off things.

David Beckham in early 1998.

The only place I've been where they have ever been polite is Ireland. If you're walking through an airport and you don't want to sign an autograph or pose for a picture, they will walk away and leave you in peace.

David Beckham.

When I was 19, 20, I was going out with Dani Behr [TV presenter] and it sort of doubled the exposure. I was down in London, photographers were chasing us in cars and I just didn't like it. The relationship ended anyway. It was nothing to do with that, but I didn't like it, full stop. I probably made a conscious effort not to do it. And I am lucky in the respect that I lived in the area that I grew up in and I have the same friends.

Ryan Giggs.

I think I've attained such a level of celebrity status that cinema can only lessen it.

Eric Cantona, who turned to acting after football.

When you're 19, 20, you enjoy the attention, but thank God David Beckham came along to take the pressure off.

Ryan Giggs.

More than 500 journalists from more than a dozen countries will be covering the event, along with 32 television services – 15 of them live.

A Real Madrid statement on the coverage of David Beckham being officially presented to the team.

You know, I got thousands of Valentine's cards, 6,000 of them one year, and all the fan mail. I'd go to book-signings, and there'd be roads blocked and traffic jams on the M4. I never really thought about it. Now I look back and … I miss it a little bit. Yeah. I'd best be careful what I say here, but I do, a little bit. I don't want to go back there now, but it was fun at the time. It was exciting.

Ryan Giggs.

My agent was right when he said we could put my name on stair rods and sell them to people in bungalows.

George Best.

DUNCAN EDWARDS

The 1958 World Cup series brought glory to Brazil and a 17-year-old wonder man named Pele. But I often wonder, would it have been a different story for Brazil, and especially for Pele, had he been playing against our superstar Duncan Edwards?
Frank Taylor, journalist, who survived the Munich disaster.

I think Manchester United is the greatest club in the world, Mr Busby. I'd give anything to play for your team.
Duncan Edwards.

The Kohinoor Diamond amongst our Crown Jewels.
Jimmy Murphy, Manchester United's assistant manager. *The Kohinoor Diamond was once the largest known diamond in the world.*

Every manager goes through life looking for one great player, praying he'll find one. I was more lucky than most. I found two – Big Duncan and George Best. I suppose in their own ways they both died, didn't they?
Sir Matt Busby.

When I used to hear Muhammad Ali proclaim to the world that he was the greatest, I used to smile. You see, the greatest of them all was an English footballer named Duncan Edwards.
Jimmy Murphy.

The only relaxation I wanted from football was to play more football and that, I feel sure, is the only way to learn this, the greatest game in the world.
Duncan Edwards.

He was of nice disposition and sound character. He was a born footballer. He would come to school with a tennis ball in his pocket and kick it about the asphalt playground. I thought then that if he could control a tennis ball like he did, he might one day play at Wembley. He was a good, quiet lad, with no bounce about him.

Alderman JS Marlow, then mayor of Dudley, after Duncan Edwards died.

It was in the character and spirit of Edwards that I saw the true revival of British football.

Walter Winterbottom, the former England manager.

It's so tragic. Duncan hung on so long. I think we all thought he was going to live.

Wolves director Arthur Oakley. Edwards died two weeks after the Munich crash.

A truly amazing boy who, apart from being a great footballer, devoted his life to sport and supported all manners of good living.

Sir Matt Busby on Edwards at the unveiling of a memorial window to him in St. Francis' Church in Dudley.

He fought with all the unforgettable fury of that unconquerable spirit. And when he died a great sigh went round the sports fields. It was as though a young Colossus had been taken from our midst.

Frank Taylor.

Kid Dynamite, the Baby Giant, the Gentle Giant, Big Dunc, the Boy with the Heart of a Man.

Some of Duncan Edwards's nicknames.

I never had to teach my boy to play football the way Bobby Charlton's mother did. He was just born with the ability.

Sarah Ann Edwards, mother of Duncan.

This big lad came up to me at the start of the game and said, 'reputations mean nothing to me and if you come near me I'll kick you over the stand'. And that's just what he tried to do as soon as I got the ball. United beat us 5-2 in that game. What a team they had – and what a player that big lad Duncan was. He was a nice lad, too, for all his size and power. After the game he came up to me and said, 'it was a pleasure playing against you'.

Jackie Milburn, the former Newcastle United striker.

It was my very great privilege as a young lad to play in the same team as Duncan Edwards and for those who never saw him, let me add that he was without argument the greatest player I ever saw. Duncan simply had everything any footballer could wish for, and yet, with it all, he was a gentleman.

Sir Bobby Charlton on what would have been Duncan Edwards' 50th birthday.

Duncan Edwards is still the greatest player I have ever seen. He had everything. He could strike a ball with both feet, he was a great header of the ball and he could drop his shoulder like Bobby Charlton. If United were getting beat, he could play centre-forward. If we were under the cosh, he could play at centre-half. In 1966 Duncan Edwards would have been 29. He died at a criminally young age.

Nobby Stiles.

He was not just a player. He was a team.

Jimmy Murphy.

THE HISTORY OF TOM SMITH

It was on a trip to Paris, in 1840 that an adventurous and forward thinking Tom Smith discovered the 'bon bon' sugared almond, wrapped in a twist of tissue paper. Seven years later this simple idea evolved into the Christmas Cracker.

By placing a small love motto in the tissue paper he created enormous interest in this product, especially at Christmas and it was during a search for inspiration to achieve even greater sales that he casually threw a log on the fire. The crackle sound, made by the burning log, gave him the idea that would eventually lead to the crackers we know and love today. After a great deal of hard work and experimentation he came up with a cracking mechanism that created a 'pop' as the "bon bon" wrapping was broken. This eventually became the snap and the cracker was born.

Over the next few years his idea evolved and grew and he moved from his original premises in Clerkenwell, East London, to Finsbury Square, in the City. His sons, Tom, Walter and Henry took over the business when he died and later a drinking fountain was erected in Finsbury Square, by Walter, in memory of his mother and to commemorate the life of the man who invented the Christmas Cracker.

It was Walter who introduced the paper hats and he toured the world to find new and unusual ideas for the gifts.

The company was very aware of current affairs and crackers were created for the Suffragettes, War Heroes, Charlie Chaplin, The Coronation and many other great occasions. Exclusive crackers were also made for the Royal Family and still are to this day.

DEDICATION

People think there are degrees of loyalty. There's no degrees of loyalty. If someone lets me down once there's no way back.

Sir Alex Ferguson.

Denis was my hero. When I was a player, I tried to copy him. The way he wore his sleeves, the way he wiped his nose, everything. To me, Denis epitomised everything a Scotsman was. One, he could start a row in an empty house and fight his shadow. Two, he loved chasing lost causes. To me he represented what a real Scotsman was.

Sir Alex Ferguson on Denis Law.

When I left school at 16, I made the conscious decision that I would cut myself off from all of my mates. It sounds brutal, and it was selfish, but I knew that they would be doing all sorts of teenage things that I couldn't get involved with, even if it was just having a few drinks out in Bury.

Gary Neville.

Cantona had his faults, he had a million faults, and was his own man. But the biggest thing he did at our club was hit home the importance of practice to attain perfection.

Sir Alex Ferguson.

At the end of the game you're knackered, and there are times when you come out of the shower when you feel you can hardly walk. But if I came off the pitch and I didn't feel like that, I'd feel as if I'd cheated myself by not trying or running my hardest. But I don't ever feel like I need a rest. I just love playing.

Wayne Rooney.

They know I'm right. They know you can't achieve anything by being lax in your life.
Sir Alex Ferguson on his players.

Maybe some unknown soul in my dressing room may unconsciously say, 'I've made it.' Well he's in for a shock.
Sir Alex Ferguson replying when asked if any of the players might rest on their laurels after winning the Treble.

If anyone thinks that all the things David has accomplished have landed in his lap, they couldn't be more wrong. Since his formative years he has practised from morning until night. You won't find anyone more dedicated. David can do absolutely anything with a football. He deserves all the success he has achieved so far and, believe me, there is more to come in the future.
Eric Harrison, former youth team coach, in 2001.

Of all the people I've handled as a manager, Ole Gunnar [Solskjaer] is the closest thing to the perfect professional that I have ever had. Not just in his demeanour as a professional footballer and the way he goes about his life but the way he understands and accepts professional football.
Sir Alex Ferguson.

The crowd enjoy it when you're tackling, they cheer you when you do a good block. To get that sort of applause as a defender in Italy, you'd have to run past five different people and finish up scoring a goal. Here, they appreciate you for fighting for every challenge.
Mikael Silvestre.

I judge a good player on whether they have been doing it for eight, nine or 10 years, not one. And there are plenty who have had one good season, then disappeared because they think they have arrived. They should focus on what they're doing in training, in the gym, what they're eating, who they're hanging around with, whether they're resting enough. Manchester United should be 24 hours a day and nothing else should come into it. Unfortunately with younger players nowadays as soon as they've played 10 or 15 matches, all of sudden they get their decent contract, their agent, and they can slack off. They lose five per cent but that's enough because it's such a fine line between winning trophies and not.
Roy Keane.

People talk about the great fighting traditions of Arsenal but no other club has a greater tradition for that than Manchester United.
Sir Alex Ferguson after the epic victory over Arsenal in the 1999 FA Cup semi-final.

We never gave up, but the time to give up is when you are dead. The time to reflect is when you are in a coffin, not on the football field.
Sir Alex Ferguson after the same game.

I've four years left of a six-year contract, but the way I look at it is you are repaying the club every day. That is Gary Neville's way.
Gary Neville.

This club is not about egos. It's not about breaking records but maintaining the tradition and success that Sir Matt Busby achieved. When players have achieved and left this club – people like Bruce, Pallister and Hughes – they can reflect on what a great time they had. The rest of us don't: we just have to carry on. I always liken it to a bus. We're going on to the next stop and if anyone is left behind, it's their own fault.
Sir Alex Ferguson after winning the Premiership in 1999.

You are always certain of getting close to 100 per cent from him. You can put the kettle on by Denis.

Sir Alex Ferguson on Denis Irwin.

I can improve every part of my game. I'm always seeing things that Dwight does, Andy does, Teddy does, Giggsy does, that I can't do yet.

Ole Gunnar Solskjaer.

He was 150% fit because he wanted to be. That's the difference between certain human beings.

Sir Alex Ferguson on Roy Keane, who played the final match of the 1999 Premiership campaign with an injured ankle.

I always try to find something to improve in every match. I have to try to be perfect.

Park Ji-Sung.

Personally I don't like playing a slow game, pushing the ball around. It seems to me like kicking a man when he's down, making fun of the opposition. I suppose this is why I don't think of foreigners as being professionals in the same sense as us. They're not prepared to give everything in the same way as our fellows.

Sir Bobby Charlton.

If I get on a bike, I feel that I could win the Tour de France. Anything is possible if you put your mind to it.

Eric Cantona.

PHILOSOPHY

Winning isn't everything. There should be no conceit in victory and no despair in defeat.
Sir Matt Busby.

When seagulls follow the trawler, it is because they think that sardines will be thrown into the sea.
Eric Cantona.

If a Frenchman goes on about seagulls, trawlers and sardines, he's called a philosopher. I'd be called a short Scottish bum talking rubbish.
Gordon Strachan.

Cantona free, philosophy nil.
Daily Telegraph headline on Eric Cantona's famous seagulls quote uttered after he had his two – week prison sentence reduced to 120 hours of community service for his kung-fu attack on a Crystal Palace fan.

In football, there is never the last piece of the jigsaw. You are always chasing the rainbow, no matter how successful you are.
Sir Alex Ferguson.

Nihil Sine Labore. (Nothing without work).
The motto hanging on the wall of Sir Alex Ferguson's office.

The salmon that idles its way downstream will never leap the waterfall.
Eric Cantona.

Only thing that goes with the flow are dead fish.
Roy Keane.

Jose understands winning and losing are twins in a way. You have to deal with them in the same way. When you win, you don't gloat and when you lose, you don't go bananas.
Sir Alex Ferguson after United beat Jose Mourinho's Chelsea to the 2007 Premiership title.

Who am I more scared of – the gaffer or my missus? Neither. Always have your alibi ready – that's my motto.
Roy Keane.

If you live on your past glories, I don't think you get anywhere. When you are trying to climb a mountain, you don't do it looking down.
Ole Gunnar Solskjaer.

I feel awkward saying, 'we'll murder 'em,' and those kind of things. This is a dangerous game to go around boasting in.
Dave Sexton.

Don't go looking for glory otherwise it will pass you by. Let it come. Work for it.
Malcolm Musgrove, assistant manager to Frank O'Farrell.

They know on the Continent that European football without the English is like a hot dog without mustard.
Sir Bobby Charlton

When players get through into goal scoring positions, they think of too many things. I always say, 'when in doubt, blast it'.
Sir Alex Ferguson.

DECLINE

They'd done it, they were proud and they had every reason to be. And then they sat back and you could almost hear the energy and ambition sighing out of the club. It was not that the willingness to win had disappeared completely. It was still there. But after the European Cup it didn't seem quite so important. It was like being in at the winding-up of a company.

George Best.

Words cannot describe how sick I feel at this moment. I can't believe this has happened, but I know it has.

Tommy Docherty after United were relegated.

I blame myself partly because I brought a lot of the players to the club and recently we have not had as much success with youngsters.

Joe Armstrong, scout, on the same event.

It was disappointing to go down but towards the end of the season a pattern of play began to emerge again and this gives us confidence for the future.

Sir Matt Busby.

In all my forty years as a player, manager and director, I've never been in the Second Division. It's a terrible disappointment.

Sir Matt Busby.

Being wise after the event, I would say that relegation was a blessing in disguise.

Sir Matt Busby.

While I was there the foundations of a once great club were eaten away by internal squabbling. Team spirit vanished and players went into revolt. The club was rife with petty jealousies, an unfriendly, almost hostile place to be. There were players who hardly bothered to talk to me or acknowledge that I was around the place. Bobby Charlton and George Best, for instance, they were great performers, but I lost respect for them. They would not talk to each other off the park and during the game seldom passed to each other.

Ted MacDougall, the former United striker.

Teams used to have three men marking George. In the end they didn't bother to stick a man on him.

Malcolm Musgrove, assistant manager to Frank O'Farrell.

It was the worst Manchester United side I have played against in ten years. There was no method about the team and they rarely came out of defence, with even striker Brian Kidd playing back on the edge of his own penalty area. United have enthusiasm, but it is not to win, just to avoid being beaten and I feel sorry for them in many way because they have to live up to the old United tradition.

Tommy Smith, Liverpool full-back, in 1973.

They are one or two players short and some of those they've got need a good talking-to.

Bob Paisley, the then Liverpool manager, on United in the early 80s.

FERGIE

Alex Ferguson shakes me up and screams at me now and again. He is like my mother or my father. He sets my limits and my aims.
Cristiano Ronaldo.

When he is happy and calm he speaks to you well. He treats you like a son. But when he is angry, I don't understand him!
Juan Sebastian Veron.

Putting it into words is very hard. For me it's been an honour, a pleasure. What he's done for this club, it will be years and years before we appreciate it. Not necessarily the team, but the structure of the club, the training facilities, the young kids coming through. The foundations are fantastic and it's all down to him. Then there's the five or six lads who have come through and are in the England team.
Roy Keane.

I owe Sir Alex a lot; people who don't know him stitch him up but he's always got a smile, a laugh or a song for everyone. He sings all the time.
Jesper Blomqvist.

He has this smile which makes the players feel so good.
Fabien Barthez.

I've played under many England managers, but nobody comes close to Sir Alex. He's helped me incredibly, he's so loyal to his players. People say he's a hard man and he is, but he's fair with it. If you do well you can ask him for anything. His office is always open for football and personal matters.
Phil Neville.

People outside Old Trafford have no real idea how much of a perfectionist Sir Alex is. To this day I am convinced he has some way of measuring the grass. But then he leaves nothing, absolutely nothing, to chance.

Keith Kent, former United head groundsman

We couldn't have been more fortunate to be at this club with this manager. He gave us our opportunity, which many people will say now – looking back – that it was the easy thing to do, because there was so much obvious ability in the lads. But it was a very courageous decision, and a lot of us owe our opportunity to him. He's been the biggest factor in the success over the last ten years at this club, with the continuity and his control from top to bottom.

Gary Neville.

I'll be celebrating all week! Seriously, no matter what kind of differences we have, this is a fantastic achievement. I don't know all the history, but he's certainly one of the greatest British managers, with what he's done. Of course I respect him for that.

Arsene Wenger on Sir Alex's landmark of 1,000 games in charge of United.

Like most of his former players, I miss being around his workplace. He's got a great sense of fun. You'd often hear him singing in his office or as he walked down the corridor, some stupid song from a musical or a 1950s film.

Peter Schmeichel.

Alex Ferguson is a threat to my son. Sven told me during a phone conversation that it is pointless having national team games in April or May because Ferguson, in one way or another, makes sure his stars aren't fit.

Ulla Eriksson, Sven-Goran Eriksson's Mum.

He terrified us. I'd never been afraid of anyone before but he was such a frightening bastard from the start. Everything was focused towards his goals. Time didn't matter to him; he never wore a watch. If he wanted something done he'd stay as late as it took or come in early. He always joined in with us in training and would have us playing in the dark until his five-a-side team won. He was ferocious, elbowing and kicking.

Bobby McCulley, former East Stirlingshire forward.

He made me captain at just 17 and was always fantastic with me. I've heard all about his reputation now but he never threw teacups at me or anyone else but he had a very young team and it wasn't necessary. He is one of those people with an aura about him – you could just feel it. I think he's one of those great figures we see running through history; he's definitely got the gift of leadership.

Tony Fitzpatrick, former St Mirren captain and then manager.

He is very black and white. If he doesn't like you, you've got to do a lot to change his opinion. But if he does like you, you'd have to do a lot to upset him.

Alan Curbishley.

He is helping me to improve because I am a bad loser. When I lose I am not very keen to be with other people. He showed me a lot of respect and quality in that sense. He was in his office waiting for me and my staff with a bottle of wine I gave him before the game. He lost a semi-final and that feeling is not good but he was there completely open and respectful. When I have this kind of teacher then one day when I lose, I must open my doors for the winner.

Jose Mourinho after Chelsea knocked United out of the Carling Cup.

He's a gent from Monday to Friday. Then on Saturday out comes the beast.

Paul Ince.

I was scared to death of him the first time I met him. I still am actually.
Paul Scholes.

I'll never forget Sir Alex Ferguson. At Christmas, everyone was
invited to a dinner, and the manager and his coaching staff all
worked as waiters. I was served by Ferguson himself. Nobody back
home believes me when I tell them this.
Diego Forlan.

I've always admired him. He's a football man, he likes players, he
loves the game. When you played against United you always felt
you wanted to impress him. Not because you wanted to sign for
them but because he was the man, the Godfather.
Graeme Le Saux.

When we meet in an airport or Uefa meetings we don't fight. Those
meetings are even funny. When there is no match, we have exciting
talks about football. There is no bitterness. I don't know the man,
but I respect the coach.
Arsene Wenger.

He's a leader of men. That's what he does best and it wouldn't
have mattered where or when he managed a club like United, he
would have been successful. He just gave players so much belief
and even when we played Real Madrid in that Cup-Winners' Cup
final he wasn't fazed at all and made sure we weren't either. His
enormous mental strength is unquestionable.
**Alex McLeish, Rangers manager and former Aberdeen centre-half,
under Sir Alex.**

After a reserve game at Forfar, he was shouting and wagging his finger at one of the boys. In his anger he kicked the laundry basket and these pants flew through the air and landed on another guy's head like a hat. He didn't move. Just sat there rigid. Fergie didn't even notice until he had finished raging. Then he looked up at the boy and said, 'and you can take those f****** pants off your head. What the hell do you think you're playing at'.

Mark McGee recalling an incident when he was one of Alex Ferguson's players at Aberdeen.

I once rang him up and was on for 10 minutes about players and he told me about every player, their strengths and their weaknesses. I put the phone down and I said, 'I bet he even knows the Dunfermline groundsman,' so I rang him back and said, 'hey Alex, I forgot to ask you about the Dunfermline groundsman' and by God he did know his name and where he came from!

Neil Warnock.

After a bad game you know the fans hate you, but Fergie used to make you think he hated you. You felt like crying and often he wouldn't speak to you for five days. But you just had to get on with it. But it has made the people who have worked under him a lot stronger mentally. A lot of the time it was a test, because if you cracked it became obvious that you couldn't handle it at the top.

Gordon Strachan.

A thousand games at the same club is incredible, incredible, fantastic. You must be a top manager and love football, and the club must love him and the players must love him because when you are so many years in the club, if the players don't like you they cannot bear to see you when you arrive in the morning. 1,000 games for me – naah. I will be in the Algarve before then. At 55, Algarve for sure.

Jose Mourinho.

CRITICISM

Glory, believing the publicity, had cost us. Rolex watches, garages full of cars, mansions, set up for life – then forgot about the game and lost the hunger that got you the Rolex, the cars and the mansion.

Roy Keane lays into his underachieving United team-mates in his autobiography.

When you go into print and criticise a player you're also risking the relationship with their family. If I criticise my players, 'that bloody Beckham, that Keane, he's a bloody idiot, been sent off, I'm fed up with his behaviour, I'll sort him out,' that type of thing, the mother's not happy with that. The father, his brothers, his pals, you make enemies of people.

Sir Alex Ferguson.

I still remember Steve Bruce ripping me to shreds at Elland Road, Mark Hughes charging at me just because I hadn't played the ball into the channel, Eric Cantona giving me the stare, Keaney and Incey snarling. And that was before you had to face the manager. It was a hard school, but the best education imaginable.

Gary Neville.

Teddy Boys.

Bob Lord, then chairman of Burnley, on United in the George Best era.

I think when people boo you it's a sign of respect, really.

David Beckham.

When I do criticise the club nowadays, it's the response of a supporter and not an ex-manager.

Tommy Docherty.

DECISIONS

Everyone knows that for us to get awarded a penalty we need a certificate from the Pope and a personal letter from the Queen.
Sir Alex Ferguson.

It was an instinct. Nothing else. You smell danger and that depth of feeling burns inside and tells you precisely the next move. I had to discard poor old Jim – the man I gave a debut to way back in 1978 – for the sake of Manchester United. There was no other decision ever in my mind.
Sir Alex Ferguson on dropping goalkeeper Jim Leighton for the FA Cup final replay against Crystal Palace in 1990.

Don't even dare ask. Just don't ask me
Jim Leighton to journalists.

I only know one way to take penalties; to score them.
Eric Cantona.

To get a penalty at Old Trafford, Jaap Stam needs to take out a machine gun and riddle you full of bullets and even then there will probably be a debate over whether you were shot inside the penalty box or just outside.
Paolo Di Canio, then at West Ham.

You need to shoot somebody with a Tommy gun to get a penalty in a big game.
Sir Alex Ferguson.

The Doc wasn't scared of the big names; he'd drop the Lou Macaris and the Stuart Pearsons and give the kids a chance.
Jimmy Nicholl, the former United defender, on Tommy Docherty.

DEBUTS

I scored on my debut, turned round and the first to come and celebrate was Eric [Cantona]. That was special.

Ole Gunnar Solskjaer.

This was brilliant. This was a different dimension. This was why I came here.

Dwight Yorke after scoring twice on his home debut for United.

When I made my debut the boss said, 'Ryan, you're on the left.' Eric couldn't have written a better poem than that.

Ryan Giggs.

I found myself laughing out loud because it was like watching a fairy tale.

Wilf McGuinness, former player and manager, on Wayne Rooney's debut against Fenerbahce.

I'd never experienced anything like it, 63,000 people at Maine Road, roaring, the noise was unreal. And the game was unbelievable. City in them days were fantastic. Summerbee, Bell, Lee, and Mike Doyle at the back, who always used to stir up derby games by talking about how he hated United. It was three apiece, and I was lucky enough to get the first goal for United. George had said, 'if you score today Sammy, there's a bottle of champagne for you'.

Sammy McIlroy.

The main memory I have of that day is when the manager read out the team about an hour and a half before kick-off and said my name! I always try to listen at the gaffer's team talks but I wasn't too sure what he'd said at that point. I thought I'd have been one of the subs, but from then on I was pretty nervous up until kick-off. I think my goal was an own goal and if it had happened in this day and age, I think it would be down as an o.g. But the record books say it's my goal, so I'll take it!

Ryan Giggs.

I came on as a sub for Willie Morgan against Cardiff in the old Second Division four days after signing. It was 0-0 and I was so frightened the first time I got the ball that I just crossed it. Stuart Pearson, who'd lent me some boots, scored. I had a hand in another goal and we won 4-0. It was beyond a fairy tale. And, despite later winning trophies, that day was my highlight as a United player. My heart was jumping out of my chest, I've never had another experience like it. I wasn't running, I was floating across the grass. Words don't do the experience justice. I've had a few operations and it was like that little pleasant stage after the anaesthetic. Only multiplied by 100.

Steve Coppell.

I had been training with the first team and playing well in the reserves but never gave myself a chance of a game. I remember sitting there terrified that I might get on. Next thing I know, I have taken Andrei's [Kanchelskis] place! I've still got the shirt.

David Beckham, who came on as a sub in the League Cup game against Brighton in 1992.

It looks like the fans have a new hero. It was a marvellous debut, almost unbelievable. I felt his penetration could make a difference for us.

Sir Alex Ferguson on Cristiano Ronaldo.

LOSING

One five-nothing defeat is a lot better than five one-nothings.
Sir Alex Ferguson after losing 5-0 to Newcastle.

The Cantona situation cost us everything.
**Sir Alex Ferguson after losing the 1995 FA Cup final to Everton.
United also failed to win the Premiership in the season Eric Cantona
was banned.**

We created so many chances at the end that I wish I was still
centre-forward.
**Sir Alex Ferguson after the 1-1 draw with West Ham that cost
United the Premiership title in 1995.**

I was driving to work and you see the kids smiling on their way to
school. In your blinkered way you think how can they be enjoying
themselves? What can there possibly be to smile about on a day
like this? But you get over it.
**Sir Alex Ferguson the morning after losing to Fenerbahce in the
Champions' League.**

In the end we were accused of bottling it. I'm not admitting to that –
but we've never made any excuses and I'm not going to start now.
**Steve Bruce after losing the old First Division title to Leeds United in
1992.**

Defeat at Bournemouth was a horrible experience. Funnily enough,
we beat Barcelona not long after in the Cup Winners' Cup and I
told Maradona that he could think himself lucky he hadn't been
playing Bournemouth.
Ron Atkinson after being knocked of the FA Cup by Bournemouth.

I used to come home in a hump if we got beat. Now I see Thomas smiling and it changes everything. There's only room for one baby in the house.

Paul Ince.

Having worked so hard to get yourself through the rounds to the final, losing is one of the biggest disappointments you can feel in football. You feel devastated and totally drained, both physically and mentally. Last year was an experience that I never want to be faced with again.

Denis Irwin after losing the 1995 FA Cup final.

I don't play against a particular team. I play to fight against the idea of losing.

Eric Cantona.

Some setbacks don't just numb you, they smack you right between the eyes and leave a vacuum in your life, a void that just seems inescapable.

Sir Alex Ferguson after United failed to win the First Division title in 1992.

Too many of our players thought all they had to do was turn up to collect their medals. And they did – loser's medals.

Martin Buchan on United's FA Cup final defeat against Southampton in 1976.

To lose after that was like winning the pools only to find you'd forgotten to post the coupon.

Sammy McIlroy after United's last-minute FA Cup final defeat by Arsenal in 1979.

I have never come across the situation we had in the closing weeks of that season. Our failure seemed to make a lot of people very happy. I find it difficult to understand. It is bitter and twisted.

Sir Alex Ferguson reflecting on United's near miss for the title in 1992.

I have seldom felt so depressed in my life as I did that weekend.

Denis Law after scoring the goal for Manchester City that sent United into the Second Division.

We murdered Everton – it could have been 22-4. They had three chances and scored four.

Ron Atkinson after United lost 4-2 to Everton.

At times like this I wonder if I should open the dressing room door and let the fans tell the players exactly how I feel. Quite simply, they have underachieved. They have received a rollicking – and quite rightly so.

Alex Ferguson after United lost to City, 3-1, in 2002.

I don't honestly know what was going through the minds of the players but I left them in no doubt what was going through mine.

Sir Alex Ferguson after the same game.

I was ashamed. I felt like jumping off the cliffs of Bournemouth.

Ron Atkinson after United lost to Bournemouth in the FA Cup.

It makes me feel physically sick to see other teams parading trophies.

Roy Keane.

When United lose I feel solely responsible. Things get too much for me. My brain will go mad. I have a storm in my head and the noise inside is deafening. It takes a lot out of me. At times I just feel numb.

Ruud van Nistelrooy.

At the moment I must confess my overwhelming mood is that I have let the fans down, betrayed them almost. But we must not allow ourselves to think about title failure over so many years as a curse. We must not believe the world is against us.

Sir Alex Ferguson after failing to win the First Division in 1992.

I believe that when Manchester United are beaten, the whole country, apart from United's fans, celebrate. It's like the people's triumph.

Paolo di Canio.

It was probably the worst thing that has happened in my career. There were careers on the line after that game because if you are not performing, the manager will show you the door. I can't describe how I felt in the dressing room. It wasn't just the result but the performance. People questioned our hunger and desire after the game but everyone tried their hardest, we just didn't perform well at all.

Phil Neville after losing 3-1 to Man City in November 2002.

I was at my lowest ebb since the Munich air crash and it was in my mind to turn my back on football altogether. It seemed the fates had conspired against the club and myself.

Sir Matt Busby after being knocked out of the European Cup by Partizan Belgrade.

My drive has never been about the buzz of winning. I'm driven by the fear of disappointment and losing. The winning buzz fades quickly. The main thrill is making it to the top. When you're there, it's like, OK great, but what now? You go on holiday and by the time you return, it's all forgotten. Those empty summers where I've sat on the beach thinking about missed opportunities have been horrible. They are what stick in my mind, more so than the wins.

Ryan Giggs.

I need the thoughts of the disappointments to spur me.

Roy Keane.

You know things never go on for ever and at some point, some time … but if it's going to happen I hope it's long after I'm in the big penalty box in the sky, in peace.

Sir Alex Ferguson on United's unbeaten home record in Europe.

If they finish second they've flopped.

Ron Atkinson on United.

COMINGS & GOINGS

It's amazing how easily it all ends, you just pick your boots up, move on and then probably don't bump into the lads until you're in town or something.

Denis Irwin.

Sir Alex has been great. He sent my wife a lovely bunch of flowers and he sent me a quid for a pint.

Brian Kidd, Sir Alex Ferguson's assistant, after he left United to manage Blackburn Rovers.

It was the day Stalin died. But, for Manchester United fans, the more important news was the signing of the Barnsley centre-forward, Tommy Taylor.
Stephen F Kelly, author. The date was March 5th, 1953.

When I told the rest of my team-mates in the Dutch squad that I was joining United next season, they were all really enthusiastic. They all stood up and applauded me into the dining room.
Ruud van Nistelrooy.

I never thought I'd spend this amount of money.
Sir Alex Ferguson after signing Juan Veron for £28.1 million.

It was time to go, it was time to part and the problem is when you fall in love with one of your players because of what they've done with you. Players almost become like family but when you get to that age then you have to make that terrible decision and change things.
Sir Alex Ferguson on Roy Keane.

I can't begin to understand what must have been going through someone's mind when they choose Blackburn and Newcastle over United.
Gary Neville.

A lot I've done since leaving has been to prove Alex Ferguson wrong.
Paul McGrath, the former United defender.

Big Ron From Old Swan Signs On.
Message on T-shirts doing the rounds of Liverpool after Ron Atkinson was sacked. Atkinson comes from the Old Swan area of Liverpool.

When he was playing in Russia he was earning £2 a month. Last year we paid him £350,000. What does he want?

Sir Alex Ferguson after Andrei Kanchelskis' request for a transfer.

I just don't understand him. But perhaps the problem is that he can't understand the questions of the Scottish reporters.

Sir Alex Ferguson on reports that Andrei Kanchelskis wanted to join Glasgow Rangers.

My heart is with United but I can't stay for one reason, and that's the manager.

Andrei Kanchelskis.

I could never criticise them. United gave me four excellent seasons and nothing will ever change that.

Andrei Kanchelskis in 2001.

Old Trafford, win or lose, is a place you hate leaving. The ground and Manchester United are like a disease – once into your bloodstream there is no escaping their charm and passion for good football.

Bryan Robson.

Every signing you make is a gamble – even if it's for five bob.

Sir Alex Ferguson.

It's a vital stage in my career. If I was just going to be sitting on the bench or be part of the squad I would stagnate a little bit. The animal in me says I have got to play on.

Steve Bruce explaining why he left United to join Birmingham City.

I'd been over there since leaving school and it was a sad day when I had to pack my bags.

David McCreery on leaving Old Trafford.

Sell Bobby Charlton? I would as soon sell myself.

Sir Matt Busby.

In the past few days I have signed up for more money than I've earned in all my fourteen years as a footballer.

Charlie Mitten, who left United and signed for the Santa Fe club in Colombia in 1950.

When I signed him from Shrewsbury [Town] for £100,000, Harry Gregg said, 'You've got a player who doesn't know the meaning of defeat'. A week later I phoned Harry back and said, 'Aye, and defeat's not the only word he doesn't know the meaning of. There's passing, control, dribble ...'

Tommy Docherty on Jim Holton.

He has found his spiritual home.

Sir Alex Ferguson on Eric Cantona

One minute we're thinking: he's an ugly, French, one eye-browed git, then he crosses the Pennines and becomes a dark, brooding, Heathcliff-type.

United fan after Eric Cantona signed for United.

We're just very grateful he's here. He's such a great player. I'm still pinching myself. A player like that only comes along once or twice in a lifetime, and you don't leave him out or put him in the reserves. You respect his skill. Eric is the brainiest player I've seen, he sees such a lot when he is on the ball and this team is perfectly suited to him.

Sir Bobby Charlton on Eric Cantona

He's the player to light up our stadium.

Sir Alex Ferguson after signing Eric Cantona.

When I asked about Eric's [Cantona] availability I wasn't worrying about his temperament. I was trying to bring a huge talent to Old Trafford.

Sir Alex Ferguson.

I'm definitely not interested.

Malcolm Allison, then Manchester City boss, after George Best was put on the transfer list.

It's a tragedy so much talent is going unharnessed.

Ron Saunders, then Norwich City manager, on the same event.

He loves wheeling and dealing, but he's not in the Ron Atkinson mould, with a chequebook as big as his ego. He's always looking for a bargain – an uncut diamond he can polish.

Jim White, journalist, on Sir Alex Ferguson.

Let's be honest, Alan Shearer knew he would've been a little fish in a big pond at Old Trafford.

A United fan after Alan Shearer signed for Newcastle rather than United.

Ex-Manchester United players are meant to have wings on their feet or something.

Francis Burns, the former left-back.

I don't sign centre-halves with earrings.

Ron Atkinson to Paul McGrath.

Half a million for Remi Moses? You could get the original Moses and the tablets for that price.

Tommy Docherty.

It's the kind of problem I wouldn't like to inherit, let alone buy.

Joe Mercer, then Coventry boss, after United put George Best up for sale.

He's like Steve Coppell with tricks.

Ron Atkinson after he signed Jesper Olsen.

I didn't want to go to Manchester, because I liked it at Parma. But Parma's coach decided he couldn't fit me into his new system.

Jesper Blomqvist.

Because £12 million is all I could squeeze out of the Scottish git.

John Gregory, Villa boss, explaining why he didn't hold out for more from Sir Alex Ferguson when transferring Dwight Yorke from Aston Villa to United.

I ended up shaking John Gregory's hand when I left and he gave me a big hug. Then I read in the papers the next day that if he'd had a gun he would have shot me and I was stunned.

Dwight Yorke.

When it comes to transfers, it's not what you pay, it's what you get.
Sir Alex Ferguson.

You can't go on believing one day you're going to get chosen ahead of Juan Veron.
Colin Murdock, a former United youth player, who moved to Preston.

There were other European clubs interested but my mind was made up. I might be American, but even I know you never say no to Manchester United.
Jonathan Spector.

Every signing you make is a gamble. But look at Andy's goal record. Some people would pay £10m for that.
Sir Alex Ferguson after signing Andy Cole for £7m.

Never, never, never, never, not now, not ever.
Real Madrid president Florentine Perez on speculation that David Beckham would move to Real Madrid.

It was weird, like stepping from London into Coronation Street.
David Beckham on his move to Manchester from London.

It feels good to come and play for such a big club. I may not start every match, but it feels like a fun thing.
Henrik Larsson after joining United on loan.

I have heard that a lot of strikers have come here and struggled. But I'm here to enjoy myself and that is exactly what I intend to do.
Dwight Yorke.

You should always buy when you are winning.
Sir Alex Ferguson.

When I saw Sir Alex at the airport I thought to myself, 'here is the biggest coach in the world coming to meet me at the airport, with a big smile on his face'. It's something I cannot describe. I was overwhelmed.
Massimo Taibi.

F*** off, I've got a pub to run and goats to feed.
Andy Goram to Sir Alex Ferguson, who phoned to inquire about signing him. Goram thought the call was a wind up by Ally McCoist.

I got Roy Keane to Manchester United. Alex called me at the time and asked what I thought about Roy Keane. I told Alex to get him bought. He said Forest wanted too much money and I said in another year or two you will be able to flog him off to Europe for four of five times that. I told Alex that he had got an engine on him like you would never believe and that he would run all day. The next day United went out and bought him.
Jack Charlton.

Every time I join a new team, I am like a writer starting with a blank page.
Eric Cantona.

It didn't have anything to do with the price tag or the expectation and I was never in awe of United. Admittedly the stadium was fantastic and you could play five-a-side in the restaurant. But I never felt intimidated by it all.
Garry Birtles.

People wondered how I would adjust. But Old Trafford folk drink tea and eat fish suppers as well, you know. Why people should think it's all champagne and caviar beats me.

Lou Macari.

After ten years at Luton, they are the only club in the world I would have left for in my testimonial year.

Mal Donaghy.

When I signed for Manchester United everyone said I wasn't worth two bob let alone £7 million. It only made my shoulders broader, my determination greater.

Andy Cole.

Coming here from London takes time to adjust and let's face it, everyone's wary of Cockneys.

Sir Alex Ferguson on Paul Ince.

The club has great midfield players like Bryan Robson and Paul Ince and it's up to me to show that I am worthy of a place in the first team.

Roy Keane on his British record £3.75 million transfer to United.

I don't set the prices. You've just got to find a way of getting them if you really want them.

Sir Alex Ferguson on transfers.

I didn't think he would reach the standard he has or I wouldn't have sold him. But it was a great sale at the time.

George Graham, who sold Andy Cole when boss of Arsenal.

With the aid of my mother's advice I had to make a choice and I was very tempted to go to Arsenal. Since I was a Northerner born and bred you would have thought that Highbury would be the last place for me. Yet the temptation was a very real one. Arsenal still had the tremendous glamour, even if it hasn't collected many trophies in recent years, and there's almost a physical attraction in going to a club which boasts such names as Hapgood, Bastin, James, Male and the Comptons.

Sir Bobby Charlton, then a 15-year-old, who was wanted by 18 clubs.

The humiliation could not have been bigger. At 29, I had been an automatic choice in both the United and the Dutch national side, and now I was considered too inexperienced and pushed aside for a 35-year-old Frenchman.

Jaap Stam, who left United and was replaced by Laurent Blanc.

I had a conversation with Roy Keane about it and he agreed, saying, 'they sold you like a cow'.

Jaap Stam.

But I must admit I miss the song the English fans used to sing to me, 'yip Jaap Stam is a big Dutchman'. Whenever I heard that, it would send a shiver down my spine.

Jaap Stam.

I'd rather jack it in than leave United. They're the only team I've ever wanted to play for. I'm absolutely gutted over what's happened. I'll prove to Alex Ferguson my loyalty for the club by playing for free if I have to. United have always been my first club and I've had so many years with some of the world's quality players at Old Trafford. I don't want to go anywhere and the club confirming talks with Barcelona has left me speechless. If the club don't want me that's something beyond my control, but my heart is at Old Trafford and I can't believe the way things have snowballed while I've been away.

David Beckham.

Once upon a time a manager would ask himself how many goals a potential new recruit might score. Now the question is, how many replica shirts can he sell?

John Toshack on the Beckham transfer to Real Madrid.

One of the things that made Manchester great is going. And with the togetherness that group of players had, and the things they had achieved, well, it is the beginning of a break-up for that group.

Arsene Wenger on David Beckham's move to Real Madrid

How dare he sell David Beckham? What's the world coming to?

John McEnroe.

Any player who doesn't really want to come to Manchester United needs their head examining and that's not being disrespectful to them. It is a hard decision for any footballer. But to me Manchester United is the only choice and that's above any other club in the world.

Roy Keane on Ronaldinho, who turned down a move to United.

I read what Roy Keane said and I think he has made a big mistake. His comments went too far. United are not the only club in the world. There are a lot of others in the same class and in my opinion one of them is Barcelona.

Ronaldinho.

Ronaldo is not just a footballer, he is waiting to be an icon. He would enhance any team, any league anywhere. I really believe he is that good.

Eusebio, the former Benfica and Portugal great, on Cristiano Ronaldo.

After we played Sporting [Lisbon] last week the lads talked about him constantly and on the plane back from the game urged me to sign him. That's how highly they rate him.

Sir Alex Ferguson on Cristiano Ronaldo.

In my consideration, Manchester United are the greatest club in the world and for that reason I picked them. I feel it's a great joy, but it's also a great responsibility. I hope to answer everything that's asked of me and I hope that everybody is proud of me.

Cristiano Ronaldo.

I can't remember the players being so excited about a new player since we signed Eric Cantona.

Ryan Giggs on Cristiano Ronaldo.

I was on very good terms with Sir Alex, even at the end. He was perfect – a nice person and a great manager.

Diego Forlan.

When he tells me it is time to move on, I will shake his hand and go without any animosity. People forget he has been like a second father to me; it is a relationship that goes beyond that of the normal player and manager.

Phil Neville on Sir Alex Ferguson.

No player who plays at this club should ever be stupid enough to think the grass is greener elsewhere because it isn't. I have listened to players who have left this club over the last five years or so and have never heard anyone say they enjoy it more than they did when they were playing at Manchester United.

Gary Neville.

The chance of replacing Peter was the main bait for me to come to Manchester United – not something I was frightened of. I could not have found myself sitting in Italy or Spain having turned down the chance to follow Peter Schmeichel. I could not have looked at myself in the mirror if I had done that, but I am not as good a goalkeeper as him.

Mark Bosnich.

I'm not bothered where he has gone, not bothered at all. If I had wanted to know where he was going I would have made sure I knew. I would have made a stipulation about where he was going.

Sir Alex Ferguson after Mark Bosnich joined Chelsea.

He said he felt he had become a pawn of United's merchandising department and that he was not going to accept such treatment any longer. His second complaint was that United were not ambitious enough in the purchase of players. I had a lot of sympathy with him on both counts.

Sir Alex Ferguson explaining the reasons for Eric Cantona's departure.

I thought, 'Who are Manchester United?' No one had heard of them.

Charlie Mitten recalling being approached by the club in 1935.

When you've been here for a few years and you experience what you experience, the thought of going somewhere else and not feeling the same about the club and not enjoying the friendships you have here doesn't bear thinking about.

Gary Neville.

To think Sir Alex Ferguson pinpointed me is staggering. I'm humbled by it. This is something I never imagined would happen.

Tim Howard after he signed for United.

My only doubts were when I got off the train in Manchester and all the buildings were black. But when I asked Jimmy Murphy [Sir Matt Busby's assistant] where the ground was and he said Trafford Park, it sounded nice. It wasn't quite what I imagined.

Sir Bobby Charlton on his arrival in Manchester to sign for United in 1953.

I wasn't just up for sale, I'd been carted as far as the check-out.

David Beckham on hearing the news that Manchester United wanted to offload him.

There were no boot deals, no car, nothing, absolutely zilch, man. I once got put on the transfer list for asking Matt Busby for a five-bob-a-week rise.

Denis Law.

Wayne Rooney is a good player but I have to be sincere and say what has been paid for him is crazy.

Rafa Benitez.

I've got the best player this country has produced since George Best.

Sir Alex Ferguson on Wayne Rooney.

Apparently a couple of Liverpool directors had been watching me. Then halfway through my second year at Liverpool University I got a call telling me that Manchester United wanted to buy me and that Tranmere had agreed a fee. It was like a dream. I told Tommy Docherty that I had an option to delay my studies. He said, 'absolutely no chance, football can be finished at the click of your finger, academic qualifications are with you for life'. I'm eternally thankful for that. Docherty was a major influence on my life and I still love him to bits.

Steve Coppell, who was a full-time economics student when he signed for United.

I remember Alex Ferguson saying to me when I first signed, 'you won't believe what it's like to play for Man United'. And I was like, 'Yeah, yeah, yeah'. But he was right, you're not used to anything like it. It was a fantastic atmosphere up there. Probably the most welcoming club I've played at. I experienced both sides of him. I don't think I ever got the hairdryer but I was on the receiving end of his wrath. But he's a warm man and a fantastic manager.

Teddy Sheringham.

It hurt a lot. Everyone knows I'm a Man United fan, Man U mad. I signed for Real Madrid and, when I got home, I cried. I expected to stay there my whole career. People were saying I was already talking to Real Madrid. I never talked to them until I got the call to say the club wanted to sell me.

David Beckham.

It is a dream the size of the world.

Anderson after signing for United.

There was only one emotion filling my mind the day I joined Manchester United. It wasn't quite in the proportions of sheer terror, but I was scared, definitely scared.
Andy Cole.

For the players he left behind at Manchester United, there will be one lasting memory of Garry Birtles. His weird, way-out gear ... the fancy bow-ties, winged collars and spectacular suits that nobody else would wear without the courage of four bottles of wine.
Steve Coppell.

I don't think contracts mean anything to Eric. If he wants to walk out he probably will do.
Martin Edwards, then United chairman, on Cantona.

I want to stop while there is still petrol in the tank. I don't want to be kicked out.
Peter Schmeichel.

At the end of the day all I can say is that I never wanted to leave Manchester United.
Paul Ince.

At first, it was a shattering blow. I cried for a week.
George Switzer, who was released by United when he was 19.

I would like to publicly thank Sir Alex Ferguson for making me the player I am today. I will always hold precious memories of my time at Manchester United and Old Trafford as well as the players, who I regard as part of my family, and the brilliant fans who have given me so much support over the years and continue to do so.
David Beckham as he left United for Real Madrid.

I've known David since he was 11 years of age, and it's been a pleasure to see him grow and develop into the player he has become. David has been an integral part of all the successes that Manchester United have achieved in the last decade. I would like to wish him and his family every success in the future, and thank him for his service to the club.

Sir Alex Ferguson.

You're going to the only place madder than Manchester United.

Sir Alex Ferguson to Patrick Harveson, who quit as the club's director of communications to work for Prince Charles.

The Londoners are different, you know. I think it's something in the water down there, you know, so at times Sheringham can be a little bit flash. Incey was a bit flash, but once he got settled in he was all right. Beckham's a Londoner, he's a bit flash at times. I think it's the make-up of the London people to be honest. But once Sheringham got up here, we could control him a bit better.

Sir Alex Ferguson.

ERIC CANTONA

Eric is really encouraging. He doesn't say much. He just winks and that gives me all the encouragement I need.

David Beckham in 1996.

Of all the many qualities a good team must possess, the supreme essential for me is penetration. And Eric brought the can-opener.

Sir Alex Ferguson.

Collar turned up, back straight, chest stuck out, he glided into the arena as if he owned the f***ing place. Any arena, but nowhere more effectively than Old Trafford. This was his stage. He loved it, the crowd loved him.

Roy Keane.

Eric Cantona has a unique talent and vision and has played a significant part in the development of the young players who have come through at Old Trafford. Four or five England footballers are all the better for that.

Graham Kelly, chief executive of the Football Association.

He was born to play for United. Some players, with respected and established reputations, are cowed and broken by the size and expectations. Not Eric. He swaggered in, stuck his chest out, raised his head and surveyed everything as if to ask, 'I'm Cantona, how big are you? Are you big enough for me?'

Sir Alex Ferguson.

I don't think we should pay too much attention to the rumour that his next acting assignment will be in a new TV sitcom called, 'One Foot In The Crowd'.

Barry Norman, film critic.

As far as I'm concerned he has been the most influential figure at Old Trafford since Feb 6, 1958. You can talk about others since then, but they did not have the influence this person had. People talk over the years about the big things that have happened at Old Trafford, but you tell me one person who had the effect that he had in those five years – there isn't anyone. He was the catalyst for the whole thing coming together again.

Harry Gregg.

The ethos of the present team has all come through watching Eric. When I first started, training sessions would end and everyone would trot back in. That doesn't happen now. Everyone stays behind for extra skills practice, you very rarely see anyone leaving early, and that's all down to Eric Cantona. He improved this club so much, and he won the league for us in his first season.
Phil Neville.

I tended to model myself more on Eric Cantona. Steve [Bruce] was one of the talkers, like Incey and Robbo. Eric was quiet. It was great to have Brucey and Robbo talking to you, but Eric was the one who impressed me most. I noticed the way he prepared for games and the way he trained. I'm like that now, I suppose. If I am an influence on the younger lads it is by example. I leave the talking to Gary Neville.
Ryan Giggs.

Cantona was a winner for Manchester United and the Reds were a winner for the mercurial Frenchman. It was a golden marriage that never really returned from its honeymoon.
Stuart Mathieson, journalist.

Eric stamped on me and was sent off but I'd still pay to watch him play.
John Moncur, the former Swindon Town midfielder.

Given Cantona's intellectuality, perhaps the surest way to wind him up would be to challenge him on a philosophical basis. It may well turn out, in the fullness of time, that what [Matthew] Simmons actually shouted was, 'Eric! Your concept of individuality is grossly diluted! You fail to acknowledge the despair pendant upon the absurdity of the human predicament! Abandon your semi-consciousness! You're acquiescent and you know you are! Come and have a go if you think you're Sartian enough'!

Giles Smith, journalist. Matthew Simmons was the fan attacked by Cantona at Crystal Palace.

Neutrals are now insisting we should have one extreme of Eric without the other: the Thinker without the Thug. the Rimbaud without the Rambo side of Eric Cantona. There's no chance of that. For every backheel that makes a goal, there will always be one aimed at someone's face.

Jim Shelley, fan.

He's so mild mannered when the volcano is not erupting inside him, and very patient with the youngsters.

Sir Alex Ferguson

Truly, I've never known anything like it. They idolise him. More than they did Denis Law, even more than they did George Best.

Pat Crerand.

Eric will always do the opposite to what you expect. That's why he's such a good footballer – and why he's such a crazy or mythical character for a lot of people, but a very nice person for others who know him a little bit better. I only have words of thanks for him and respect for the great football player he is.

Jordi Cruyff.

He stands in front of the camera like he is about to take a penalty.
Etienne Chatillier, film director, during Cantona's acting debut.

He's more than just a circus act with his flicks and backheels …
Cantona has a picture of what's going on all around him, wide
vision. He can see round corners.
Wilf McGuinness, the former United player and manager.

Never mind the fact that he has exquisite touch and incredible
vision, Cantona is simply something else – sort of mystical in a
way. And I've felt the hairs on the back of my neck stand up just
watching him training.
Andy Cole.

When Eric feels an injustice, he has to prove to the whole world
that he's been wronged. He can't control his temper. That's just
part of his game.
Sir Alex Ferguson.

I'd give all the champagne I've ever drunk to have played
alongside Eric Cantona in a big European match at Old Trafford.
George Best.

Most great players have gone to Old Trafford and not been able to
live up to their reputation. But he has created a niche that will
never be forgotten.
Mark Hughes.

If I wanted to define him, I'd say that he's an island – but an island
of freedom, generosity and pride.
Gerard Houllier.

BECKHAM

I really wish I was playing with him. I would have scored 40 goals a season in my day and all of them with my head, by the way.
Sir Alex Ferguson.

We'd be a drearier and somehow bleaker place. We'd end up needing some sort of tribal, symbolic, emblematic figure to personify us and I just don't know if David Beckham's ready for the job … yet.
Simon Schama, historian, on what might happen if the monarchy was dissolved.

Cultural architects are people who are able to change the mindset of others. They are able to break barriers, they have visions. They are self-confident and able to transfer self-confidence to other players. Beckham has grown to become a cultural architect. He has today a very great influence on the attitudes of other players.
Willi Railo, sports psychologist.

Sir Alex Ferguson once described me as a Manchester United player in an Arsenal shirt. I think it was a compliment. In which case, I look upon David Beckham as an Arsenal player in a Manchester United shirt.
Tony Adams, the former Arsenal and England defender and captain.

He is devastatingly good looking to the point where with some people you can feel a bit of jealously. But with David you just throw the towel in and go, 'Yeah, yeah'. When I first met him I didn't know whether to shake his hand or lick his face.
Robbie Williams, rock star.

Beckham's a good lad.
Diego Simeone, Argentinian midfielder who got Beckham sent off in the 1998 World Cup.

David's lovely but he's too quiet for me. I like bolshy blokes. Victoria is the boss there.

Mel C of the Spice Girls.

The fact that he [Beckham] is prepared to be so involved with his baby matters to all the young men who want to be affectionate to theirs but have no role models.

Dr. Anthony Clare, psychiatrist.

I get letters from people thinking we are going to clone David Beckham – we are not going to do that.

Ian Gibson MP, and a Labour member of parliament's select committee on science and technology, on the cloning debate.

When it came to putting a man on Marie Claire's cover for the first time, there was only one candidate – David Beckham. He represents something for every woman – father, husband, footballer, icon. In a word, he's the ultimate hero.

Marie O'Riordan, editor of Marie Claire magazine, on her decision to put David Beckham on the cover – the first man to be given such a distinction.

As far as the outside world is concerned he is a huge star, that's definitely his image. Maybe that's because of his wife and how they live. But that's definitely not the Beckham I know as a player in my team. He is very modest when he's in the group, even shy and he doesn't like publicity at all. When he is interviewed on television and he sees it, he switches the TV off like he is ashamed of it.

Ruud van Nistelrooy.

Part of his appeal is his femininity and this is what is on display at the moment. I particularly like the fact that he is happy to be a gay icon and that he has such a sweet nature.That's what we all love him for.

Martin Amis, novelist.

To be honest, I'm not a great Beckham fan. I've talked to a lot of full-backs of my era who say they would have their easiest afternoon ever against him. That's not quite fair, because he doesn't try to be a winger. He's got a wonderful right foot but I don't consider him to be a world-class player. Someone asked me to compare him to Johnny Haynes, and I said one's Stoke Newington and the other's Mayfair.

George Cohen, England's World Cup-winning full-back.

Beckham is a great man, a great player. He can play at Inter Milan or at Real Madrid but if I was Manchester United I would never let him leave. He knows how to play football like no-one else.

Sven-Goran Eriksson.

That was the most phenomenal entrance I have ever seen. They are sooooo Hollywood, so glam and over-the-top. They are the new Ben Affleck and J-Lo. They were just so amazing, totally tasteless but glam and so bling, bling, bling.

Steven Cojocaru of People Magazine after Posh and Becks attended the MTV Movie Awards in Hollywood.

He's the best footballer in the world and she's really beautiful.

Samuel L Jackson, actor, on Posh and Becks at the same event.

The guy's my hero. I think he's absolutely gorgeous. Everyone is smitten with Becks and Posh.

Beyonce, singer, at the same event.

They're a nice couple and he's so talented.

Harrison Ford, actor, at the same event

He's an amazingly talented guy. She's very beautiful.

George Lucas, film director.

Don't Come Beck

Besides a spectacular free-kick in a desperate game against lowly rated Greece, his [international] achievements have been extremely modest. [Last week] it was leaked that Beckham would be appointed OBE in the next honours list. That gives him equal ranking with the late Bobby Moore, who won England's only World Cup in 1966, an achievement that touched the nation. This is the deep problem with the Beckham story. It is evidence that the value of real achievement has been profoundly diminished.

James Lawton, journalist.

When you get into the back of his car, he says, 'don't scuff me levver'. We're always imitating him, but he doesn't mind, he just laughs.

Ryan Giggs on Beckham during their early days at United.

Beckham is far too handsome to be a footballer. I don't know whether to kick him or kiss him.

Juan Veron.

This Gaultier-saronged, Posh Spiced, Cool Britannia, look-at-me, what-a-lad, loadsamoney, sex-and-shopping, fame-schooled, daytime TV, over-coiffed twerp did not, of course, mean any harm.

Part of an editorial in the Daily Telegraph after Beckham was sent off in the 1998 World Cup.

"So, tell me, is your little boy starting to put whole sentences together?"
"Yeah, he's learning bits and pieces."
"And what about Brooklyn?"
Ali G to Victoria Beckham.

The run-up to internationals is an important time and I do find it bizarre that he draws attention to himself like this before the forthcoming England matches. From the pictures I've seen it looks absurd. I would never have a haircut like that, but then with my ears I would look a complete prat.

Gary Lineker, broadcaster, on a new David Beckham hairstyle.

He's more Albert Square rather than Rover's Return, more pie and mash than Betty's Hot pot.

The Daily Star.

I call what he does football competitions. I can never remember what they're supposed to be.

Victoria Beckham.

It's very difficult to pick out a youngster. It's an art, and one that I have no gift for, but when I saw David Beckham it was quite obvious that he was going to make it. A lot of players want to be footballers but I've never known anyone that wanted to be one more, and was preparted to work as hard as David Beckham to become a success

Sir Bobby Charlton.

I used to love it when the punters had a go at me. I got awful stick, with some vile abuse being hurled at me from the terraces. But I got a buzz out of it. David has got to shove it up them.

George Best.

If they ever start cloning footballers, he'd be the first one you'd send to the laboratory.

Kevin Keegan.

Beckham cannot kick with his left foot, can't head the ball, can't tackle and he doesn't score enough goals. Otherwise he's all right.

George Best

GEORGE BEST

Maradona good; Pele better; George Best.
Banner at Best's funeral.

In February 1961 he took a 15-year-old Belfast boy on to his playing staff, and although he didn't know it at the time, by doing so he achieved his ambition and fulfilled his dream. The boy's name was George Best and from the moment he signed for United nothing was the same again, not for Sir Matt, nor the club, and most certainly not for George Best.
Michael Parkinson.

As in any programme about Best, the most enjoyable bits of This Is Your Life were the clips of him playing football. Like most footie enthusiasts of my age, I am practically a PhD on the subject of old TV footage of George Best, on and off the pitch. But there was one I didn't remember seeing before, in which – in a blur of miraculous footwork – he stopped the ball going into touch, controlled it, nutmegged an opponent and skipped round him. It was like watching Rodin chiselling, or Einstein thinking. Genius at work.
Brian Viner, journalist.

George was the kind of man a lot of men would find themselves in love with.
James Nesbitt, actor.

British football is so mundane, because everyone's influenced by midfield players instead of being influenced by George Best.
Johnny Marr, rock star.

Yes, I feared for George every day of my life since the path we shared for those few, amazing years parted so sharply, but no, I didn't think to change him. I didn't presume that ability. I could ask him how he was doing, tell him that I still loved him and that the days we had together would always be precious, but George was George, unchangeable, ungovernable if you like. I'm told it is often the price of genius.

Mike Summerbee, friend and former Manchester City winger.

One huge part of his impact was that he was such a beautiful man. Another was that he was so naturally unassuming. In our nights on the town – and there were quite a number – he never saw himself as the centre of attention. If he had an entourage, it was not appointed, or created by him. It was a case of iron filings attaching themselves to a magnet.

Mike Summerbee.

He has left us with a million memories, all of them good ones.

Sir Alex Ferguson.

He is the kind of person that never dies. What they leave behind doesn't disappear. I can see, for example, my kids in 10 years' time watching a George Best video.

Jose Mourinho.

To me, he was one of the finest players in the world, not just of his generation but of all time. He was a lovely man as well.

Kim Book, the Northampton Town goalkeeper beaten six times by Best in a FA Cup fourth-round tie in 1970.

Cruyff was manufactured on Earth. George Best was made in Heaven.

Derek Dougan.

I walked down the streets of Manchester with him and saw the girls flock to him; girls of all ages, office workers in mini-skirts and bouffant hair, and old ladies with walking sticks. I saw the traffic stop. I saw that the world was invading George in a way that went far beyond football. A club like United, who were aware of what an asset they had, were also invaded by this new attention, this crazy onset of celebrity. They had no adequate defences.

Mike Summerbee.

If I'd known then what I know now I'd have given him a right smack, but at the time we all had enough on our own plates without trying to solve his problems.

Denis Law.

If we'd known then what we know now, it might have been different. We at Manchester United have learned from our experience with Eric Cantona. We had to treat him a lot differently, make allowances. If, instead of being hostile to George, which I was, we had leaned a bit his way and tried to help him, who knows?

Sir Bobby Charlton.

George was the most naturally gifted player I have ever seen. He had the lot: balance, pace, two good feet, he was brave, strong and a good header of the ball. Pele wasn't as gifted as George Best. He couldn't beat players in as many ways as George could. And I would definitely put George above Cruyff, because he had more heart. Maradona would be close, because he was more of a team man.

Johnny Giles.

Feet as sensitive as a pickpocket's hands.

Hugh McIlvanney, journalist.

Some people are just born with a craft and leave an indelible mark on people's lives. The thing I remember, apart from his talent, was his courage. I can see him flying down the wing riding tackles from people like Ron Harris, Tommy Smith and Norman Hunter. They were serious guys – you didn't mess with them – and it was a time when you needed to be struck down by a tomahawk just to get booked, yet he rode all that. Every time he went down he got up again and just said, 'Give me the ball'. That will stick in my mind forever.

Sir Alex Ferguson.

George was the first superstar of a league in which everybody now thinks he is a superstar. He bequeathed the keys to hundreds of sleek sports cars and mock Tudor mansions to mere mortals. Best was the advance party to the discovery of paradise, the player who transported footballers' faces from cigarette cards to bedroom walls and billboards. The original version.

Clive Tyldesley, broadcaster.

He carried us for years, it was an honour to carry him.

Derek Dougan, one of Best's former Northern Ireland team-mates and a pall-bearer at his funeral.

I always felt his presence and the importance he had at United. But the past was not a burden. It carried us. It was a reference point, something we could lean on.

Eric Cantona.

I still marvel at Best's six goals against Northampton in the FA Cup. You think about doing that in a parks game but not in the FA Cup against a side who could kick a bit. Unfortunately his rare talent was allowed to fade before its time. When he looks at how Alex Ferguson has handled the likes of Cantona, I wonder whether he regrets that someone did not handle him in the same way.

Bobby Gould.

Nobody can take away from his genius. That is undisputed. Yet I found George someone with great compassion and humanity. I recall him going to hospital with me to see a young fan and presenting him with a signed programme and the jersey which he wore at Windsor Park when he took Scotland apart by himself!

Malcolm Brodie, Northern Irish sports journalist.

I recall him helping me to celebrate my first-team debut in 1971. After the game against Man City he bought me a bottle of champagne which I kept for years before opening, as he had bought it. In that era of greats – such as Cruyff and Pele – he stands alongside them.

Sammy McIlroy.

If George had been born ugly he probably would have played till he was 40 ... just look at Peter Beardsley.

Pat Crerand.

He was the best player I ever attempted to kick in 21 years.

Chopper Harris, the former Chelsea hard man.

He is as brave as a VC winner

Sir Bobby Charlton.

People say he wasted his career. Nonsense, he was hunted down by defenders for 11 full seasons, starting at 17. He paid his dues all right.

David Meek, journalist.

He should have been captain and more respected as a footballer, because he's an intelligent lad, not the fool that people take him for.

Eamon Dunphy, journalist.

He is a son of instinct rather than logic.

Geoffrey Green, journalist.

Every day there was a story in the papers about George Best – but most of the things we were reading were not about what he had done on the field, but about sleeping with three Miss Worlds or whatever. I cancelled the Daily Mirror, because I was sick to death of reading all their stories about George.

Jack Charlton.

I live in hope that one day I'll go along to a youth match, as in 1963, watch an unknown kid for five minutes and find myself asking, 'my God – who is that?'

Pat Crerand on the search for another Best.

Looking back I feel guilty. George Best was a youngster when he came into a great side and I don't think we senior players took enough interest in him. Older players influenced me a great deal when I was young, but we failed to influence George Best.

Bill Foulkes, the former United defender.

They should show the kids films of his matches. They'd learn more from five minutes of George than they would from five years of coaching videos.

Pat Jennings, the former Spurs, Arsenal and Northern Ireland goalkeeper.

The only thing I have in common with George Best is that we came from the same place, play for the same club and were discovered by the same man.

Norman Whiteside.

I remember one game where Best glided past Harris' waist-high tackle, struck the ball through Marvin Hinton's legs, sent Eddie McCreadie one way and Bonetti the other before scoring. If he'd only gone past nightclubs the way he did defenders.

Wilf McGuinness, former United manager, after a game against Chelsea.

The bewildering repertoire of feints and swerves, sudden stops and demoralising spurts, exploited a freakish elasticity of limb and torso, tremendous physical strength and balance that would have made Isaac Newton decide he might as well have eaten the apple.

Hugh McIlvanney.

Sir Stanley Matthews should be looking over his shoulder. His reputation as the finest entertainer in British soccer is in danger of being overhauled. By, of course, George Best of Manchester United.

Sir Tom Finney early in Best's career.

Let him alone. Don't try and coach him. The boy is special.

Sir Matt Busby's advice to the training staff at Old Trafford after Best arrived.

He had ice in his veins, warmth in his heart and timing and balance in his feet.

Danny Blanchflower, the former Spurs and Northern Ireland captain.

We had problems with the wee feller, but I prefer to remember his genius.

Sir Matt Busby.

My only reaction upon hearing that George Best had been named Footballer of the Year by claiming 60 per cent of the vote was to ask my informant,'who on earth did the remaining 40 per cent vote for?'

Michael Parkinson after Best became Footballer of the Year in 1968.

George Best knows he let a lot of people down a lot of times. But what he also did was to make people's dreams come true.

Denis Law.

George is full of good resolutions and good intentions, but he must learn that it is not enough to give them. You have to keep them.

Frank O'Farrell, the former United manager.

If George Best were an Englishman we would keep the World Cup for the next 10 years.

Sir Bobby Charlton.

George thought he was the James Bond of soccer. He had everything he wanted and he pleased himself. He had money, girls and tremendous publicity. He lived from day to day. Until right at the end he got away with it when he missed training or ran away. So he didn't care. People made excuses for him; he didn't even have to bother to do it himself.

People talked about pressures and depressions. it was rubbish. He just hadn't any responsibilities, nothing to worry about at all. All kinds of people covered up for him, even the Press, and he was lucky to get away with it for so long.

Willie Morgan.

They don't come any greater than George. I never had a cross word with him, the most ordinary superstar you could meet. No airs or graces, no sort of ego about him.

Jeff Stelling, Sky Sports presenter.

Maybe people criticise him for the way he led his life but, if he had never led his life like that, maybe he wouldn't have been the player he was.

Kenny Dalglish.

John Lennon made a joke once about being a legend in his lunch hour. George Best was probably the first player to become and then remain a legend throughout his lifetime.

Hunter Davies, journalist.

He was such a great player he could get away with almost anything and that was a mistake. He should have been kept on a tighter rein. He was strong, athletic, good tackler, good in the air and could score goals. He had everything when at his peak.

Tommy Docherty.

BLIMEY

When he takes his position in the goal, he doesn't shine through demeanour or size. But when the match starts, it's the metamorphosis. The man, always in short sleeves, liberates an enormous energy, a devastating violence. He flies, he soars, he hovers like an extraterrestial.

Aimé Jacquet, French football coach, on Fabien Barthez.

Unconsciously, I fell in love with a small round sphere with its amusing and capricious rebounds, which sometimes play with me.
Fabien Barthez.

Hey, even if it's in the middle of the game. How often do you get a chance to talk to Jaap Stam? So if there's a free-kick or a corner, I might go up to the United players and say, 'so, do you like Singapore?'
Aide Iskandar, Singapore player, before a pre-season game against United.

The goalkeeper plays a key part in the game. He is not there only to stop balls. He gives rhythm and intensity to the game.
Fabien Barthez.

I thought Larry White was someone else.
Laurent Blanc on his nickname among United supporters.

He's a beer-burger-brothel-bomber – and he likes to shoot in the dark.
German tabloid Das Bild on Wayne Rooney.

I exploded [at the Carling Cup final against Wigan] and began swearing at Ferguson because I felt he had kicked my soul. That was the moment things died and, after that, things would never be good, they could never be the same again.
Ruud van Nistlerooy on his row with Sir Alex Ferguson at the 2006 Carling Cup final when he wasn't even used as a sub. The row led to his departure from the club.

Norman's [Whiteside] greatest quality has always been his quality.
Ron Atkinson.

When I score a fantastic goal I celebrate it with a death leap. I hope to be able to do it many times in the Premiership.

Nani, United's new signing from Sporting Lisbon.

People talk about the future, but the future's now.

Roy Keane.

I always prepare myself with an Elvis song and I try to bring a little bit of his magic on to the pitch.

Ole Gunnar Solskjaer.

AFTER HOURS

In her youth the Queen was quite a stunner. Who knows what might have happened if I'd met her at Tramp in my heyday.

George Best.

I soon learnt that if you're a footballer it doesn't matter how pig-ugly you are, you will always get attention from the fittest birds.

Rio Ferdinand.

I just walk into a pub and women throw themselves at me.

Ryan Giggs.

Mary Stavin is the only woman to whom I was almost always faithful.

George Best.

I'd love to sit at a piano alongside Jerry Lee Lewis because he was the greatest piano player of all time. You can talk about Chopin, anyone. But for me, Jerry Lee Lewis was the best, he was unbelievable. A real rock 'n' roll player. He was fantastic, the best I've ever heard.
Sir Alex Ferguson.

When I see my players spending their money on clothes, at least I know where it is going. I prefer that to seeing them blow it all at the bookies or in the pub.
Sir Alex Ferguson.

George Best Edwardia Ltd.
The title of George Best's clothes shop company.

I think the players are a little bit afraid of me. I will never get close to them. I will always keep my distance. Do I socialise with them? Never have, never will.
Sir Alex Ferguson.

Tell me, Mr. Best – where did it all go wrong?
A porter who arrived in Best's hotel suite to deliver champagne where he saw £15,000 spread out on the bed and a half-naked Miss World, Mary Stavin, prancing about the room.

I honestly can't remember the last time I drank champagne. Whether it was before or during training.
Ron Atkinson.

I saw a sign saying Drink Canada Dry.
George Best explaining why he went to North America.

The drinking, gambling and discos used to amaze me. Players would ask me why I didn't join them for lunch after training. Well, I can tell you these sort of lunches didn't involve much eating.

Arnold Muhren, the former United midfielder.

How do you rate Jimmy Greaves?
The only man who could drink more than me.

George Best during a question-and-answer session.

Even after a skinful, I don't have a hangover and can still be up with the others.

Bryan Robson.

In 1969 I gave up drinking and sex. It was the worst bloody 20 minutes of my life.

George Best.

There are some unwritten rules the British public should know about. I'm not allowed to play any of my music because the rest of the team hate it. Every week it's the same story. I try to play Jesus and Mary Chain and end up being forced to listen to George Benson.

Brian McClair on life on the team bus.

I don't go to clubs, so I don't meet many people. I'm wary of anyone. I think you've got to be.

David Beckham.

I don't go anywhere unusual now. I don't go out much. I don't meet with people I don't know. I don't allow myself to be taken by surprise. I don't do anything I have any doubts about.

Roy Keane.

Some players whiled away the time by reading newspapers or books, others gathered around one table for Lou Macari's card school. More often than not the other table would be occupied by [Steve] Coppell and Martin Buchan, on which they would spread their college books.

Tommy Docherty.

I would like the girl I marry to be a virgin. It used to be one of the most important things I used to think about. Finding a girl who was a virgin. But it's almost impossible for it to work. In fact it's almost impossible to find a girl who's a virgin. My ideas must be changing though,' cos I don't feel as strongly about it as I used to. And if I did find a girl who was a virgin I probably wouldn't like her anyway.

George Best.

Manchester has got everything. Great shopping malls, cinemas, restaurants, an international airport, theatres, concert halls. I go and see a lot of bands. And when I want peace I always drive into the Lake District.

Ruud van Nistelrooy.

You played a lot of football. Do you think if you hadn't played as much football you wouldn't have been so thirsty?

Mrs Merton, BBC's spoof agony aunt, to George Best.

I don't go to as many parties as people think. I'm never at any parties three or four days before a game. I'm a quiet lad and I just stay in most of the time.

David Beckham

I was a normal healthy male. I enjoyed it as much as the next man, but nothing ever comes close to scoring goals.

George Best.

The most important player is Gary Neville, he is the great organiser. He is very social and active and organises lots of events for the players and their wives. That's very important, he keeps the group together.

Ruud van Nistelrooy.

I have often wondered and perhaps you'll tell me, George. Exactly how big is your willy?

A question from a girl to George Best during a question-and-answer session.

Phil was good, they both were. Gary was a pugnacious little cricketer, really competitive. You could definitely see more of the footballer in him than Phil, who was quietly competitive, a bit like Mark Waugh – on the outside cool and collected, on the inside burning up.

Matthew Hayden, the Australian opener, who spent a summer as a professional with Greenmount in the Bolton League and trained the Neville brothers.

I've lived like a hermit for donkeys' years, and my own social activities were practically nil.

Bill Foulkes.

I wouldn't kiss any girl if she smoked too much.

George Best.

What he gave me was like paint-stripper and I notice that he didn't have any – nor did Roman Abramovich.

Sir Alex Ferguson on the wine he was offered by Jose Mourinho after a Carling Cup semi-final at Stamford Bridge.

Footballers tend not to notice or enjoy what's around them. I remember once on a tour of Italy the coach passed the Leaning Tower of Pisa. I pointed it out, only to be told, 'shut up and deal'.

Sir Bobby Charlton.

Once I started playing football I realised I was in the perfect position for pulling birds. I had the limelight, the publicity, the money. Where could I go wrong?

George Best.

We've got matching dogs, matching watches, similar wardrobes, matching Jags. I like all that. I know it is really tacky but it makes me laugh.

Posh Spice.

We go to the cinema almost every week. Cathy and I go to the early show at around five o'clock. I get my pick'n'mix and my hot dog and ice cream. Cathy says I'm a pig.

Sir Alex Ferguson shows his wife a good time.

If you want the secret of my success with women, then don't smoke, don't take drugs and don't be too particular.

George Best.

You leave Giggsy alone. He's been playing crap since he met you.

A fan to Giggs's then girlfriend, Dani Behr.

It is irrelevant whether Giggs dates Dani Behr or Yogi Bear – provided he lights up our Saturday.

Henry Winter, journalist.

Once you get the taste of George Best you never want to taste another thing.
Angie Best in 1979

The world we live in is mad because ... I'll be honest with you, if I saw an ugly bird and she was a celebrity with loads of money, she wouldn't attract me at all.
Rio Ferdinand.

They say I've slept with seven Miss Worlds. I didn't. It was only four. I didn't turn up for the other three.
George Best.

What would you do if you weren't a footballer?
Manage the Miss World contest. I might get the four birds I missed.
Exchange between a punter and George Best during one of his roadshows.

It's like George Best once said to me: when you've had the last three Miss Worlds, then you can start talking.
Maurice Johnston, retired footballer.

If you have only one passion in life – football – and you pursue it to the exclusion of everything else, it becomes very dangerous. When you stop doing this activity it is as though you are dying. The death of that activity is a death in itself.
Eric Cantona in 2003.

Every manager should have a hobby. Mine is soccer.
Sir Matt Busby.

Acting is like a small drug, but football is big, big, big! Football is the LSD of drugs.
Eric Cantona.

I couldn't get up and mingle even if I wanted to. There's always someone who wants to start a fight. Every time I go to the gents a couple of friends have to come along as well for protection.
George Best.

I was free to paint and to live with my wife Isabelle and my dogs. But it was also time for experiments. I shaved my head to feel the fresh rain and the strength of the wind on my skull ... I was at liberty to begin a session of psychoanalysis without being called a madman.
Eric Cantona on his activities during his eight month ban.

People laugh when I say I lead a boring life, but I do. I look forward to training in the morning and having nothing to do for the rest of the day other than going home. My house is the only place I can relax, other than at training or in actual matches. I get home about 1.30 pm. Then I watch a Test match or some golf on telly. Then I relax some more, have my tea and hope there's an evening football match on telly.
Ryan Giggs.

If you want, you can always have sex. Even if you're a football player. Even the night before a match.
Juan Veron.

I've never actually been to Stringfellow's. I would never go somewhere like that.
David Beckham.

YOUTH

A young man has a right to rebel.
Eric Cantona.

Boy Best Flashes in Red Attack
The Manchester Evening News' headline after George Best's debut for United against West Brom.

I was always a dead-keen Red, and if you came from our area there was no such thing as a soccer connoisseur. None of this liberal nonsense of hoping both sides did well.
Nobby Stiles.

One spotty virgin, there's only one spotty virgin.
United supporters' song for Ryan Giggs during his early days in the first team.

Nicky Butt used to clean my boots – I'm the only black person to have a white shoeshine boy.
Paul Parker.

You don't argue with the boss. But he's kind. He treats you like his son and you can talk to him.
David Beckham

I was scared of the youth team coach when I got there. To be honest, though, when you first arrive at Man United you're scared of just about everything.
Gary Neville.

I gave up a lot when I was younger. Going out with the lads, going to parties and discos, leaving my family to come up to Manchester. It was what I wanted though, so I made my choices.

David Beckham.

My young life revolved around playing football. There was no television then and people lived by their radio sets. All the kids did was play football in the streets. You kicked a ball against the wall all the way to school, then you had a game when you got there. At mid-morning break you had another game and you kicked a ball all the way home at lunchtime, and so it went on.

Denis Law.

In those days when I was a kid the only thing I shared my bed with was a football. I used to take the ball to bed with me. I know it sounds daft but I used to love the feel of it. I used to hold it, look at it and think, 'one day you'll do everything I tell you'.

George Best.

The greatest, most fulfilling joy a manager can have is that of seeing a young boy arrive unknown, step on the field of play and then realise you have seen a great star make his debut.

Sir Matt Busby.

I had four teenagers in Aberdeen's 1983 European Cup-Winners' Cup side and none of them are still playing today. I have to ask myself, 'should I have rested them?' I don't want to make the same mistake.

Sir Alex Ferguson on blooding young players too early.

If they are good enough, they are old enough.

Sir Matt Busby.

It's very flattering when you're 14 and Alex Ferguson comes in for you. You tend to think, 'yeah'.

Ryan Giggs.

People say that it was a poor upbringing. I don't know what they mean. It was tough but it wasn't bloody poor. We maybe didn't have a television. We didn't have a car. We didn't even have a phone. But I thought I had everything and I did. I had football.

Sir Alex Ferguson.

We played in the streets mainly, or in the park. Whoever had a ball and got there first would start a game and more boys and men came and joined in until it was 20 or 30 a side. We kept it going all day long. Lunch was the only thing that would make me stop and even the men would only leave to have a drink. It wasn't just youngsters – it was all ages.

Sir Bobby Charlton.

Where I was brought up, you had to be able to run or fight and you know about my running.

Pat Crerand.

People won't believe me when I tell them I played the church organ down in the Rhondda when I was 15. I can best forget football playing Beethoven, Bach and the other great composers on the organ and piano. I like to read too – Mark Twain and Chesterton. You can learn a lot from those fellows.

Jimmy Murphy, Sir Matt Busby's assistant, in 1962.

I don't want to butter you up, Missis, but your boy will play for England before he's 21.

Joe Armstrong, United scout, to Bobby Charlton's mum in 1953.

I was a skinhead in a duffle coat and Doc Martens with my football boots in a plastic bag tucked under my arm.

How Norman Whiteside dressed when he travelled over to Old Trafford as a youth.

One of the biggest thrills of my life was when I got my first United blazer to go on a youth tour to Ireland. I stopped people to see how they thought it looked on me

Albert Scanlon.

I'm one of the few people in this world who've been across the pitch at Old Trafford on my hands and knees getting weeds out with a little dibber and a bucket. They used to put string lanes about a yard wide across the pitch and about four or five of us used to have to do the weeding. Old Scott Duncan was the manager then and he used to come behind you and if you missed a weed he used to say, 'hey, lad, come on, there's one here'.

Stan Pearson, striker who played for United before and after World War Two.

I wish I never had to grow up.

Eric Cantona.

I am going to protect Ryan all I can. I have got to be honest and say George [Best] is the role model of what to avoid with our talented kids. I use George's case as an example when I speak to parents of young footballers. Everybody wanted a piece of George. This club is a refuge for Ryan. He can come and be sheltered by us. When the time comes and he can handle it, then we won't stand in his way.

Sir Alex Ferguson.

I was almost in tears watching him perform.

Alan Smith, who used to run the Greater Manchester County Schools under-15 team, on Ryan Giggs.

In my career everything has come so fast it frightens me.

David Beckham.

I suppose it was instinct really. The difference between a good player and a great player is that great players can read the game. That's something you cannot teach a guy – he either has it or he hasn't and if he has he's halfway there. But you can't teach him to think.

Billy Behan, scout

Happy is the club which can bring on a reserve and find him a star.

Dennis Viollet, the former United striker of the 1950s and 60s.

One of the secrets' of Manchester United's success is that nearly all of us grew up together as boy footballers. We were knitted into a football family.

Roger Byrne, the United captain in the 1950s.

While you could say we've had a great ten years, there's also been a preparation for the next ten years. Because of youth we're designed to be one step ahead.

Sir Alex Ferguson.

I'm not a discoverer of players. There can be no discovery without revelation.

Bob Bishop, United's Northern Ireland scout.

He was never a kid, always a man.

Ron Atkinson on Norman Whiteside.

I have found a genius.

Bob Bishop, United's Northern Ireland scout, to Matt Busby about George Best.

I really wanted to accept because I'd always loved the game. But I stopped to assess it and asked myself what's the length of a footballer's career?

Sean Connery, who turned down Matt Busby's offer to join United.

We used the arches of a warehouse for goals; the street lights used to light the place up, and we would play until all hours.

Brian Kidd.

When Cantona was captain he led by example. He had a great attraction for the young players. He would sit and talk to them and they hung on his every word.

Sir Alex Ferguson.

Like a young cocker spaniel chasing a bit of silver paper floating on the wind.

Sir Alex Ferguson on Ryan Giggs.

Five hundred games is a bit of a milestone, but you will find a few people around United, influential ones, who were not sure I would make 50. I spent most of my teenage years waiting for rejection. I still remember my shock at being one of the 16 picked out of 200 kids in the under-11s. That letter through the post was the most unbelievable thing I had ever seen.

Gary Neville.

We used to bring him to games in London – he was our mascot at West Ham when he was 12.

Sir Alex Ferguson on David Beckham

People find it hard to believe now, but at first the Busby Babes were laughed at. Football was a game for grown men, and a hard game, too. The pitches and the balls were much worse back then and the medical facilities were nothing like they are today. You had to be fully developed and physically strong to cope, and the idea that you could build a team around raw teenagers at the top level was completely revolutionary. Matt Busby thought it was a young man's game and went on to prove it. When United won the league with that team, it changed football forever. Sir Matt would be so proud if he could see what is happening today, with academies sprouting up everywhere and players like Wayne Rooney playing for England while in their teens.

Sir Bobby Charlton.

If you stuck a girl or a ball in front of David he'd pick up the ball.

John Bullock, David Beckham's school games teacher.

We've a young Irish boy here called Best, and if he doesn't make a bloody genius I haven't seen one. It's all there; the heart, the ability, everything.

Sir Matt Busby.

I always say it's about 90% arm around the shoulder, 10% kick up the backside.

Eric Harrison, former Manchester United youth coach, on dealing with young players.

As a kid me and my mates used to go up to Bond Street and look in the windows. We were always turned away by the doorman because we looked too poor.

Rio Ferdinand.

At school I was really little and used to get booted all over the place. But I was just so determined. I didn't have many friends, I just thought: I'll show 'em. I just loved playing football and I was out playing from when I got out of school, straight over to the park without any dinner.

David Beckham.

There are a lot of people, at this club and others, who like to wrap the young lads in cotton wool. With some young players, it seems to go in one ear and out the other, so you need to grab hold of them and say, 'look, you need to listen'. That's what players used to do with me – tough love, or whatever you want to call it.

Roy Keane.

But what 19-year-old has maturity? What were you like at 19, what was I like? Jesus Christ, I was trying to start a workers' revolution in Glasgow. My mother thought I was a communist. She was down on her knees praying every night. Then I got the ultimate threat – my granny spoke to me. She said, 'Mammy thinks you're a bloody communist'. I'll be shocked if I don't do the business with that boy. I'll be totally amazed.

Alex Ferguson on criticism of Wayne Rooney.

Really he's still the same little boy lost that he was when he first came to Manchester.

Mrs. Fullaway, George Best's former landlady in Manchester.

These days you need to develop the minds of young players far more than their skills. People's lifestyles have changed. Nowadays nobody walks anywhere any more – everyone goes by car. This has softened them up not just physically but, far more importantly, mentally. People don't want to suffer pain – in fact, they don't know what it is.

Sir Alex Ferguson.

Paul was such a small boy. He always got singled out for rough treatment. Boys would queue up to kick him, but he was a sturdy little fellow. Most of the time he saw it coming and got out of the way. If he did get kicked he just walked away. There were never any tantrums.

John Duncan, Scholes' headmaster at Cardinal Langley School.

But it was still heartbreaking. I was the only child, my mum and dad were devastated. The club sent me home once every three or four weeks, to be fair, but the hardest thing was getting on the plane to come back. My dad had to push me on. He'd say, 'go back, son, and stick it out'.

Sammy McIllroy, who left his home in Northern Ireland to join United when he was a teenager.

I don't have a template as such, but there are certain things you look for in a young player. They certainly need to be courageous, they must want the ball. That will never change. At our club if you don't take the ball or you don't want it you've got no chance. You won't be able to play in that atmosphere.

Sir Alex Ferguson.

Young players in the academy now have been far more cocooned than boys in the Sixties and Seventies. Everything is done for them nowadays. They don't walk; they are driven everywhere. It probably worries people at other clubs more than us; we know how to deal with it. We don't allow them to have earrings or tattoos. We try to keep players as down to earth as we possibly can. Our coaches start on their mental preparation at nine years of age, so by the time they come to 16, they're flourishing.

Sir Alex Ferguson.

As a youngster, you felt Fergie had a real aura. You'd be walking down the corridor, see him and then turn the other way to avoid him **Danny Higginbotham.**

I was a Tottenham fan because I wanted to be different. And because of Glenn Hoddle. But all my family were United fans. **Roy Keane.**

When I've finished with football, I'll be proud to say I worked with the players at United. The thing closest to my heart are the young pups – it's lovely to see them continue to do so well. **Brian Kidd**

The great thing about coming to United as a youngster is they want you to be a man first. The footballer bit comes second. They want you to look after your parents and conduct yourself in the right way. **Ryan Giggs.**

Morning kick-off, it's fabulous. You wake up at 8, you play. It's like when you are a kid. **Fabien Barthez.**

As a child, I loved Cruyff and one evening I tore up his picture before becoming myself. **Eric Cantona.**

When you're young you fly off the handle a little bit and do silly things like concentrating on yourself and always trying to score goals. As you get older you realise it's a team game and you play more for the others than yourself. **Nicky Butt.**

I was brought up with many of them. They were going to prison, I was going to the World Cup.

Norman Whiteside on the friends he grew up with in Northern Ireland during the Troubles.

When they picked teams at school, I was always the last chosen. I used to get booted everywhere because I was really little. I didn't have many friends, really.

David Beckham.

I couldn't wear glasses to play in a proper match of course, so I developed a unique system for coping with the problem. I learned to play football with one eye closed. I kept my glasses on as long as I could, while I put on my jersey and socks and boots, but when the moment came to go on the pitch and the glasses had to come off, I used to close my right eye and keep it closed for the whole of the match. I learned to play through an entire game using only one eye and I went on doing this for years.

Denis Law, who suffered from a squint in his younger days.

You mention the word heritage and history and you can't lose that part of what you are. You see the kids here today and that's what Manchester United is about, young people. We always try to produce the best young players we can. I think the most important thing is that players have come through that particular route themselves, they're local boys. Ryan Giggs and Wes Brown are local boys who came to our school of excellence and progressed the way hopefully some of these young kids are going to. What we're trying to do all over this academy is show the history of the club, all the corridors have photographs of great players we produced ourselves. It's an incentive to them that it can be done and that any young kid coming through the books at Manchester United will get an opportunity.

Sir Alex Ferguson.

We used to play football in the garden. He used to make me stand there, and he used to tackle me and then as I got older, I used to play with him, I used to tackle him real badly and injure him. And when we were in bed at night, we used to play football with the Care Bears.

Joanne Beckham, David's sister.

He was one of my heroes. I used to sit on my dad's shoulders and watch him. I used to call him Sir Allenby de Trafford, he was a mighty centre-half.

Nobby Stiles on Allenby Chilton, the former United midfielder

I wanted to be an architect. What are you laughing for? I really did.

Denis Law.

Always be ready and willing to listen to your elders, and keep yourself fit at all times.

Sir Bobby Charlton.

BEAUTIFUL GAME

The keeper made my mind up for me by coming out so quickly, so I took the ball round him. I thought about walking it in, or stopping it on the line and kneeling down to head it in, but finally thought better of it.

George Best on his goal in the 1968 European Cup final.

I was surprised by Manchester United. Here, at Old Trafford, they are actually keeping the ball on the turf in attack, instead of thumping it all over the premises, and are running into position to receive passes.

A Sunday Chronicle report after United beat Chelsea 5-1 in 1938.

I imagine the ball to be alive, sensitive, responding to the touch of my foot, to my caresses, like a woman with the man she loves.

Eric Cantona

Ronaldo's gifted, a quick learner and he's getting more effective all the time. I love his attitude, too. He says he wants to be thought of in the same bracket as me. He'll get there, too, but he'll only ever be second best. I'm not conceding first place – I'll send him the video tapes so he can see why.

George Best on Cristiano Ronaldo.

Of course I wasn't nervous. Taking a penalty to win the Cup is what you are in the game for. If you don't feel excited by that, perhaps you should not be a professional footballer.

Eric Cantona, who scored two penalties in the 1994 FA Cup Final against Chelsea.

Every day I wake up and if there's a football game to play or watch it is like Christmas Day to me

Sir Bobby Charlton.

I never wanted Manchester United to be second to anybody. Only the best would be good enough. I had to have players who would rather play for me and for United rather than for themselves, if you understand what I mean. And I usually found what I wanted.

Sir Matt Busby.

They were the best days of my life. We used to just go out and attack teams. If somebody scored three against us we knew we'd get four. It was great just going out on the pitch. We knew we'd enjoy it.

Stuart Pearson, a United striker in the 1970s.

When I first started I did not mind the hard men too much because it gave me the chance to rubbish them with my skill. I'd go past them and they'd say, 'do that again and I'll break your f****** leg!'. And next time I'd do them again and they'd say, 'Right, I f****** warned you'. Next time I got the ball I'd stand on it and beckon them to me. I used to be like a bullfighter, inviting them to charge me. They rarely got me. I was too quick.

George Best

Shellito was taken off suffering from twisted blood.

Pat Crerand after Chelsea's full-back Ken Shellito was given the run around by George Best in a game in the 1960s.

I never subscribed to Sir Alf Ramsey's doctrine of hard running off the ball. I am a footballer – and that means having a football at my feet.

George Best.

All the best players have imagination, they see a bigger picture. I watch a game and they will play a pass and I will think, 'Bloody hell, I never saw that'. That is what a great player can do. We try to develop that here, we ask them, 'What have you got in your locker? Show us what you can do?'

Sir Alex Ferguson.

What times. What matches they were. United were always the benchmark for us, glamorous, sophisticated, packed with stars. George Best, Bobby Charlton and Denis Law. We were the pretenders, they were the kings. And we told them we wanted their crown. In those days we were an uncouth lot and tested the laws to the limits.

Billy Bremner.

When he waggled his hips he made the stanchions in the grandstand sway.

Harry Gregg on Eddie 'Snake Hips' Colman, United half-back who lost his life in the Munich disaster. 'Snake hips' referred to his trade mark body swerve.

What matters above all things is that the game should be played in the right spirit, with the utmost resource of skill and courage, with fair play and no favour, with every man playing as a member of his team and the result accepted without bitterness and conceit.

Sir Matt Busby.

I scored my first big-time goal and what a feeling I got – something I can never hope to describe. It seemed I would burst with happiness.

Liam Whelan, United inside-forward, who died in the Munich disaster.

A quick goal is one way to counter the defence-minded sides, as they have got to come out to fight back. But in exaggerated 'blanket' games such as seen in Italy, and too often in Britain these days, there is little chance for forwards. But there is a big chance that the game will be ruined as a spectacle if it is sacrificed on the altar of cold science.

Sir Matt Busby in the 1960s.

Football is not about profit and loss. It is about glory and excitement, about loyalty and legends, about local identity and family history, about skills and talents, none of which can be computed on balance sheets. Football doesn't have a product. Every year [Manchester] United fans have their ashes scattered on the turf at Old Trafford. How often do you see that happening at Tescos?

Hunter Davies, writer.

It's always been adventure and romance for United.
Pat Crerand.

That goal changed me – not as a person, but as a player. People have looked at me differently ever since.
David Beckham on the goal he scored from the halfway line against Wimbledon in the first match of the 1996/97 season.

It's one of those goals that I will look back on in a few years time and think, 'did I really do that?'
David Beckham on the same goal.

Everyone is scratching their heads in the dressing room to try and remember something similar. Pele in the 1970 World Cup is the only one.
Sir Alex Ferguson on David Beckham's goal.

I was just hanging on the back of the net thinking 'shit'.
Neil Sullivan, the Wimbledon 'keeper after Beckham's goal.

Skill is something I'll never lose. I'll have that when I'm 100.
George Best.

Why don't they pick the whole side for England? The best teams from Hungary have never beaten us like this.
Anderlecht's striker Jef Mermans after a 10-0 defeat by United in the European Cup in 1956.

We can be patient if we have to, but in the end it's our nature to try to tear the other lot to pieces.
Tommy Docherty.

An artist, in my eyes, is someone who can lighten up a dark room. I have never, and never will, find any difference between the pass from Pele to Carlos Alberto in the final of the World Cup in 1970 and the poetry of the young [Arthur] Rimbaud. There is, in each of these human manifestations, an expression of beauty which touches us and gives us a feeling of eternity.

Eric Cantona on the 1970 World Cup final when Brazil beat Italy 4-1.

He has not been staled by knocks or mud or the dragging weight of repetition. He does not make a crowd think murder; what he gives them is delight.

Arthur Hopcraft, journalist, on Sir Bobby Charlton in the 1960s.

When I'm on the field nothing gives me more pleasure than making a fool of somebody.

George Best.

The goals you saw were masterpieces of their creator's craft, jewels to set in any crown.

George Best on Brazil's goals in the 1970 World Cup.

That game in Portugal for me was something of a starting point. That was probably the occasion when I decided it was only going to get better. From that match on I actually believed there was nobody better than me. It is amazing what one performance can do.

George Best recalling United's 5-1 defeat of Benfica at the Stadium of Light in Portugal in the European Cup in 1966.

If you are going to be beaten, you don't mind if it's by the great man himself.

George Best, who came second to Pele in a worldwide poll to see who was the greatest-ever player on the planet.

Perhaps it is simply because I have got older, but the soccer scene today doesn't excite me as much as when I made my debut eight years ago. Everything was new and exciting. I believe that my job is to entertain the people who have paid money to see me play. One of the big problems with modern-day soccer is that it has become too stereotyped with everybody preoccupied with defence.
George Best in 1972

I just set off.
Ryan Giggs on his wonder goal against Arsenal in the 1999 FA Cup semi-final.

One, Two, See Ya, Beep Beep, Bye Bye, Bang!
Ron Atkinson description of Giggs' goal.

That night was full of mixed emotions for me, to be honest. I was obviously very proud to have scored the goal, but shortly afterwards I picked up an Achilles injury and I ended up leaving the ground on crutches. I didn't know the goal was anything like it was; I thought I'd picked it up about 30 yards out, beat one, maybe two men and scored. I didn't actually realise that I'd got it on the halfway line and beat three or four players until I got home and watched it on television! I do cringe a little bit when I see the celebration but sometimes when you score you just don't know what you're doing. The funny thing was the fans that ran onto the pitch were a few of my mates. It was weird seeing fans coming towards you and then the next minute getting kissed on the cheek by your mate! I think that game gave us the belief to go on and beat Juventus and eventually do the Treble.
Ryan Giggs on the same goal.

Nobody stops the ball except the goalkeeper.
Sir Matt Busby.

Footballers are surrealists because they create at the moment.
Eric Cantona.

The English people preferred a Keane tackle to a Giggs dribble.
Why? Any player can tackle, few can dribble.
Jordi Cruyff.

For men who work on the shop floor, the one highlight of their
week is to go and watch football. Matt Busby used to say you
should give that man something he can't do himself. That's why
Manchester United always play attacking football.
Sir Bobby Charlton.

When United are at their best, I am close to orgasm. It is a true
wonder.
Gianluca Vialli.

Watching him this season I've witnessed acts of manipulation of a
football that verge on the physically impossible.
Gary Lineker on Cristiano Ronaldo.

Go back through the magnificent attacking players we have had
and it is clear Manchester United is a club sprinkled with stardust.
Sir Bobby Charlton.

Whatever happened to football? Whatever happened to passing
and that sort of thing?
**Sir Bobby Charlton after England drew 0-0 with Denmark in the
1992 European Championship.**

Thank you for letting me play your beautiful football.
Eric Cantona accepting his award as PFA player of the year in 1994.

MISCELLANEOUS

My big ambition is to drive into United's training ground behind the wheel of a Reliant Robin.

Dwight Yorke.

If it hadn't been for football I think I might have got really interested in a career in the Army.

Sir Bobby Charlton.

I don't understand those players, and there are quite a few, who turn up in the latest fashions every day. The United players have a go at me and call me a scruff. I get some stick in the United dressing room because I usually turn up in slippers. I have two pairs – just soft ordinary carpet slippers – one from Marks & Spencer and the other just a cheap pair with an England flag on the front bought from the market.

Wayne Rooney.

It could be an important shirt to have in the future, that. It'll be like Hitler's helmet.

Oxford manager Jim Smith after his players were fighting for Cristiano Ronaldo's shirt following a friendly with United.

The only thing I don't understand about the English is why they are so interested in the weather. One day it's light grey, the next, it's dark grey

Eric Cantona.

When I came to Manchester from the North-east aged 15, I didn't know what a director was or what he did. My dad would have explained it as someone who didn't work.

Sir Bobby Charlton as he joined the United board.

Bryan gives you the impression that your squad is bigger than it really is.

Ron Atkinson on Bryan Robson

Teddy Sheringham: there is no better name in English football. It is a name that seems to come from a different era, before the Pauls and Lees and Jasons were even thought of; a time when men were men, footballs weighed as much as suet pudding and long shorts were worn without irony.

Laura Thompson, journalist.

I would be faced with the choice of playing for Russia, the Ukraine or Lithuania, all of which I was eligible for. It was also possible that I might be eligible for France. Someone even told me that Jackie Charlton had made enquiries to see if I had great-grandparents with Irish blood.

Andrei Kanchelskis.

I have never joined in the popular game of belittling football club directors simply because they are football directors. I have always said, look at the top when analysing clubs who have lasting success, and there you will find the original cause of the happy effect.

Sir Matt Busby.

When Martin Edwards' £11 million deal with Michael Knighton fell through in 1989, he came to me and asked me to take it over. I could have bought United there and then but I am happier being at the final as owner of Wigan. I had three or four meetings with directors Bobby Charlton, Maurice Watkins and Martin, but came to the conclusion that if I bought United, which Liverpool fan would want to buy shirts from my business, JJB Sports. In fact, it would have alienated the whole of the country except United supporters.

Dave Whelan, owner of Wigan Athletic, before the 2005 Carling Cup final.

... AND FINALLY

The only thing that is perfect about me is my perseverance.
Sir Alex Ferguson.

No matter what has happened off the field since then, no matter what people think, at the end of the day they'll remember the football. They won't remember who I dated, fights and car crashes or whatever, they won't remember any of that, because it's not important. They'll remember the football.
George Best.

I want to die at Old Trafford.
Eric Cantona.

Ken Bates has been quoted as saying that we're just a club from the slum side of Manchester. To me, Chelsea could move their stadium to the middle of Harrods and win 15 championships on the trot, and even if you moved Old Trafford to Beirut, they still wouldn't be as big as us.
Gary Neville when Bates was chairman of Chelsea.

My career trickled away, I suppose but, you know, all down the years I've been fulfilled by the fact that I played 17 times with the Busby Babes.
Kenny Morgans, who was injured in the Munich crash.

Some people called me a visionary, others a reactionary, while a few called me awkward or stubborn.
Sir Matt Busby on the club's foray into Europe despite the disapproval of the Football League.

I'm more than happy. I've all my cartilages. I've no arthritis and I'm as busy as I've ever been.

Sir Bobby Charlton in his retirement.

I'd rather be called a brat than a sage. Brats want to change what they're not happy with in life. Sages adapt and always say yes when they mean no.

Eric Cantona.

I've been lucky, you know. I'd always wanted to be a footballer but I never imagined it would turn out the way it did. I've been in the right place at the right time. I could have been twenty when I played in the World Cup, not 17 and then nobody would have paid attention to my debut. I was in the right place to score that goal at Wembley.

Norman Whiteside. 'That goal' was the winner against Everton in the 1985 FA Cup final.

The greatest time for me was always just turning up to train with the rest, and know I was a Manchester United footballer.

Shay Brennan, United full-back in the 1960s.

If I could be remembered for anything when I finished in management, it wouldn't be for all the Cups, the titles and glory. It would be for one thing – that I never deserted any one of the players I had under my control.

Sir Alex Ferguson.

Now I have my memories, something that cannot be taken away from me. And I'm happy. I'm grateful to have played for United and to have got out of that aircraft alive.

Albert Scanlon.

I've been training very hard to get cliches out of my system. But it's very difficult when you come off the pitch and a reporter is looking for a quote. It's dead easy to slip into verbal shorthand. I only say, 'football is a game of two halves' if I'm taking the piss. But the cliche that catches me out most is, 'at the end of the day'. I keep telling myself to stop saying it. I keep thinking, 'remember Brian, at the end of the day it will be 11.59 pm'.

Brian McClair.

When I finish here I feel sure that will be it. I can't see anything greater than this.

Sir Alex Ferguson.

It was a lovely shirt, richer, a purer red. I'd have to pinch myself into believing it was true, this is real, you're playing in George Best's shirt. If you've done that, it doesn't matter what you do after, does it?

Gordon Hill, United winger in the 1970s.

They were great days. I had to keep pinching myself. My only dream was to play until I dropped.

Steve Coppell.

I don't want to go down as the gentleman of football. I would rather be remembered as a good player.

Sir Bobby Charlton.

I never felt that I ever let the team down or that I let myself down on the field. A lot of things were happening off the field that maybe I would have changed. I left Manchester United with a clear conscience.

George Best.

I just love the drama of it all. People ask when am I going to quit. Good grief, I would miss all that purgatory.

Sir Alex Ferguson.

I've always had success because I've always got people to have confidence in me, players and directors. They have always done their best for me and I have always tried to do the same for them.

Sir Matt Busby.

Football in England is fundamentally different to anywhere else. It's given me a lot more than I've given it

Eric Cantona.

The most important thing is the work ethic.

Sir Alex Ferguson.

If my name is mentioned in football circles in the future, I just hope they say, 'he was a good professional'.

Martin Buchan

There is always something new to fire my enthusiasm.

Sir Alex Ferguson.

When you are building a football club you never know where you are going. It's a journey that never finishes.

Sir Alex Ferguson.

I don't think I will be remembered in 20 or 30 years. I'm not being humble, I'm just being honest.

Roy Keane.

I want to die from an overdose of love.
Eric Cantona.

I can look back and think I'm just one of the luckiest people in the world.
Roy Keane on his career.

When I look back I can only think of good things. Everything I think about Manchester United is always good.
Sir Alex Ferguson.

I get paid a lot of money to play football. I consider my life to be truly perfect.
Dwight Yorke.

Football has the ability to bring people together, it's not just a way to pass the time on a Saturday afternoon.
Juan Sebastian Veron.

It's the ultimate irony that I finished my career early through injury after all those consecutive games and being so proud of my fitness. I could look at it as a tragedy, but I feel blessed that I played so many games for such a special club like United, blessed to be so fondly remembered by so many people.
Steve Coppell.

It's just been an absolute pleasure. I love this game; it's my whole life, and it has been for as long as I can remember. Since I was a very, very little boy I wanted to be a footballer.
Sir Bobby Charlton.

All the bad days cannot wipe away the memories. And despite all the ups and downs, when I look back at my life as a whole it is impossible not to feel blessed.

George Best.

Never lose your passion, or if you do, get away quickly.

Eric Cantona.

At United there was always a lot of hype before every game. I didn't think the Forest game was any different. He has nothing to thank me for. I was just doing a job of scoring goals. I will always be grateful to him for giving me the opportunity. If it was pivotal in any way, then I am proud to have played some part.

Mark Robins, whose goal against Nottingham Forest in the FA Cup in 1990 may have saved Sir Alex Ferguson's job.

It's the ultimate pressure job but you know that and I'm delighted I accepted although I got the sack in the end.

Dave Sexton.

I really have to pich myself from time to time to remind myself that I really did played for Manchester United.

John Fitzpatrick, United defender in the 1960s and '70s.

At the end of the day the bus goes on and we don't wait for anybody.

Sir Alex Ferguson.

At the end of the day I'm just a footballer.

Ryan Giggs.